The Earthsavers

Written & Illustrated by

Sulaf Hatab
Towa Moriyama Mikami
Claudio Narciso
Matteo Narciso
Aure Ruiz Halpert
Jasper Stoneberg

Literary Direction & Editing
Julietta Eisenberg

Book Design & Art Direction
Bek Millhouse

We are all members of Pono,
a democratic, urban, outdoor,
educational program in Harlem,
New York City

pono

A journey to becoming
balanced human beings

ISBN-13: 978-0692936702 (PONO)

ISBN-10: 069293670X

Printed by CreateSpace An Amazon.com Company

It is the year 3015

and the Earth has a grave problem!!!
Companies are drilling for gas too much, and it's disturbing the planet's core. This is causing seismic activity and volcanoes that are destroying habitats. If it is not stopped, it will threaten the entire world, and maybe beyond. But there is one hope:

The Earthsavers!

A team of Superheroes who will do anything to save the Earth and its citizens!

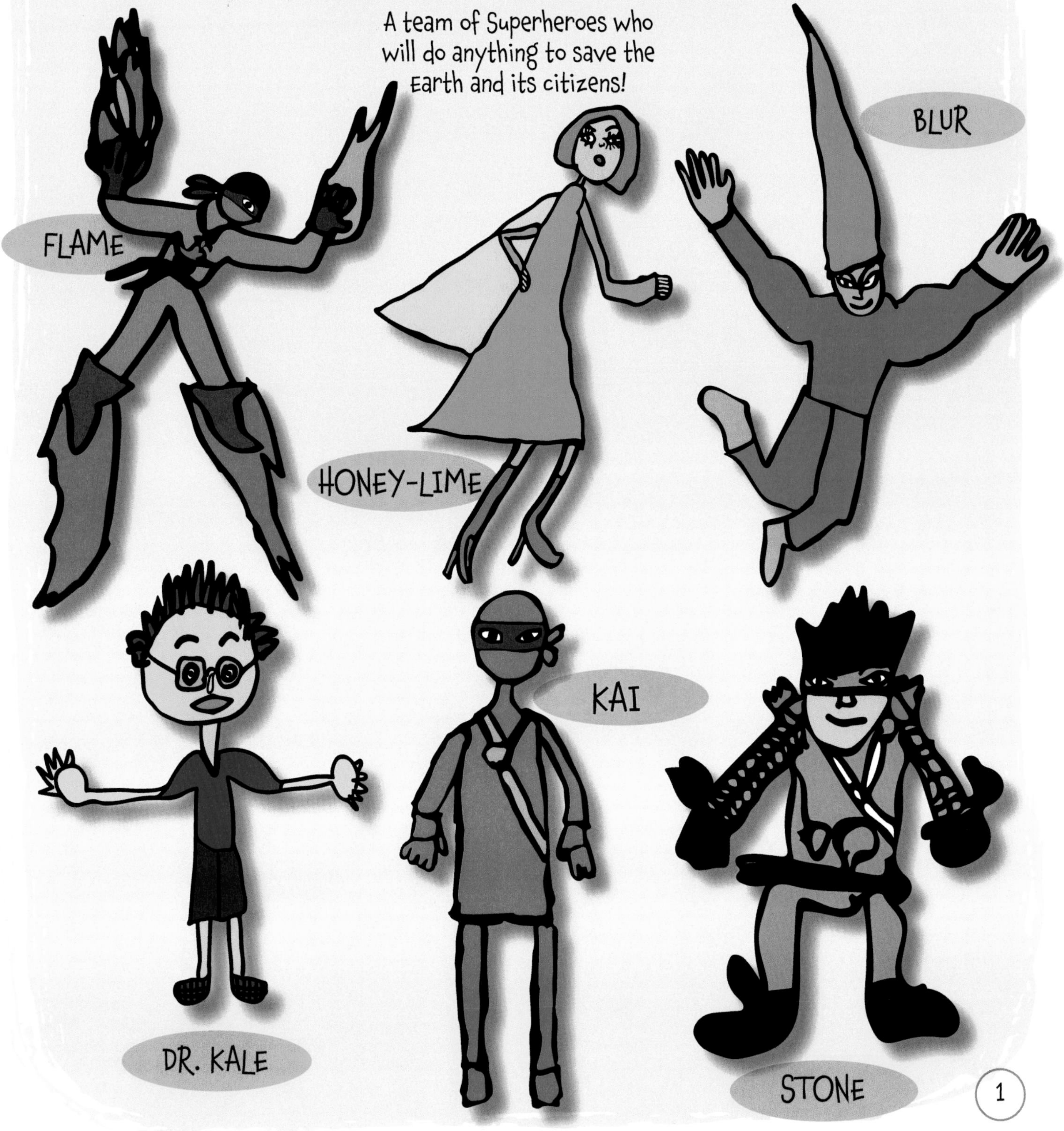

FLAME
HONEY-LIME
BLUR
DR. KALE
KAI
STONE

Introduction

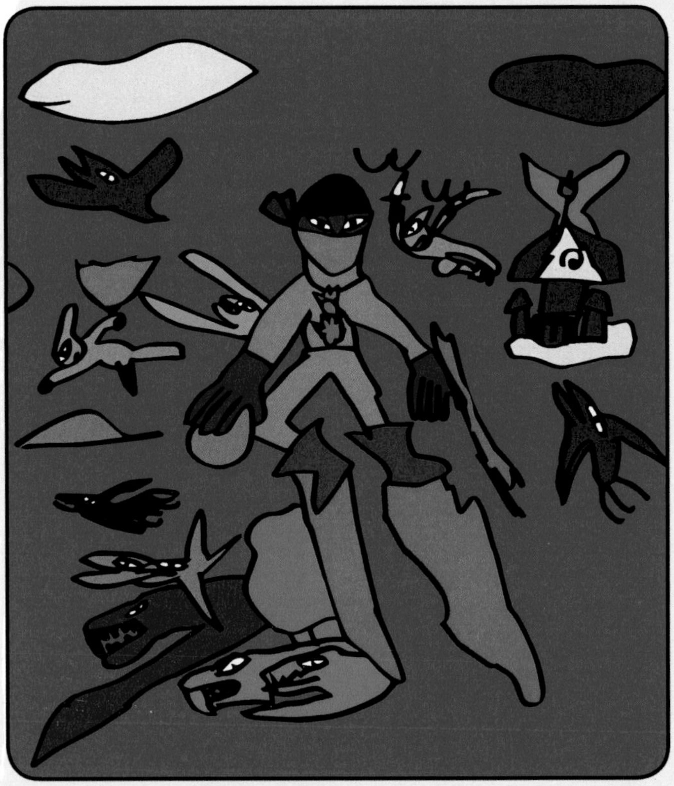

FLAME

Special Powers: Shooting fire and breaking secret codes.

Interesting facts: Shoots black flame when he is mad... He has a crush on Honey-Lime. He is patient and likes the color red. He has a pet dragon named Regasow.

Hobbies: He is a great cook and does not need matches or coal... he uses his own flames!

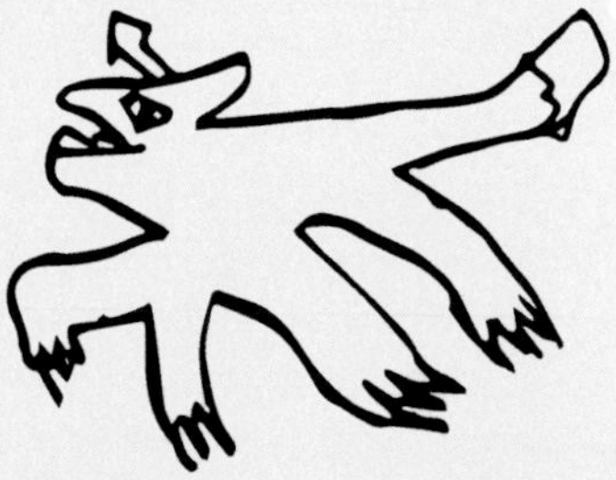

Home: Sky Palace.

Age: 300

BLUR

Special Powers: Strength and speed. Able to stop the ground from quaking.

Interesting facts: Already when he was born he could kick a soccer ball 5 miles away. When he was 12 he could kick a soccer ball 1000,000,000,000,000,000,000,000, 000,000,000,000,000,000,000,000 miles away. He is friendly, funny and sometimes silly.

Hobbies: He likes to eat spinach and always wears cool orange sneakers.

Age: 304

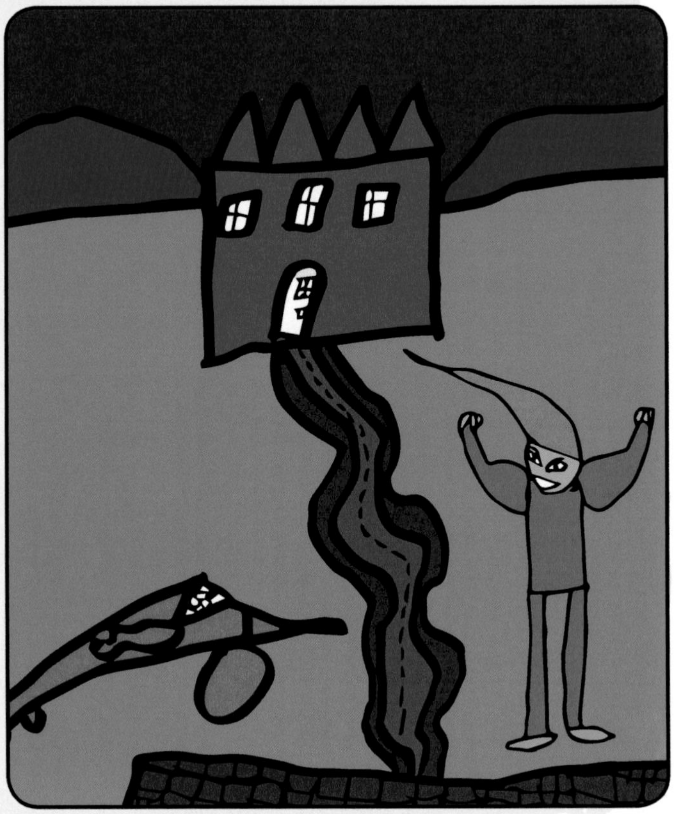

HONEY-LIME

Special Powers: Shoots liquid "agavney" (a mixture of honey and agave) from her hands. She uses her mind to talk to people far away and to get her places.

Interesting facts: Happy, confident, brave. Her favorite food is lamb's leg. Her favorite color is pink. She always wears tights.

Hobbies: Singing, belly-dancing, costume making, painting, cooking, writing and drawing. She has a pet cheetah named Maria. She loves her.

Age: 300

STONE

Special Powers: Can do anything with stone. He has liquid rock in his blood.

Interesting facts: Always gets impatient during science talks. Has a pet wolficorn. He can make rivers of liquid rock. He liked to eat charcoal as a kid.

Hobbies: Loves to eat sushi.

Age: 315

Dr. Kale's Lab

Emergency Eye Wash

DR. KALE

Special Powers: Makes medicines that cure diseases. Shoots green liquid from his arms to re-seed the Earth. Is responsible for humans living to be 900 years old.

Interesting facts: Hair changed color in a laboratory incident but he decided to keep it. Favorite Element: Protactinium

Hobbies: Playing with his cat, Ray Kufzweil and walking in the forest.

Home: Dubna, Russia

Age: 7866293000000

KAI

Special Powers: Has one lung and one gill. He breathes under water and on land. He can also meditate and create balance all around him.

Interesting facts: He lives under water in a fake volcano with one room. No one knows he lives there.

Hobbies: He likes to take naps.

Age: 33

Chapter #1
Trouble Begins

Honey-Lime is at the **Superhero Library of Global Salvation**, researching how to fix the earthquake fiasco.

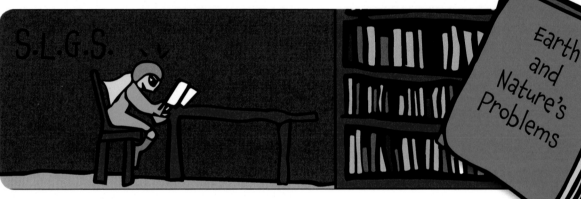

Earth and Nature's Problems

My iphone 1015 is going craaaazy. Lots of seismic activity here. Honey-Lime, help!

Oh! I'm getting a message from Dr. Kale.

Oh no! There's tectonic trouble in Pennsylvania.

WHOA!

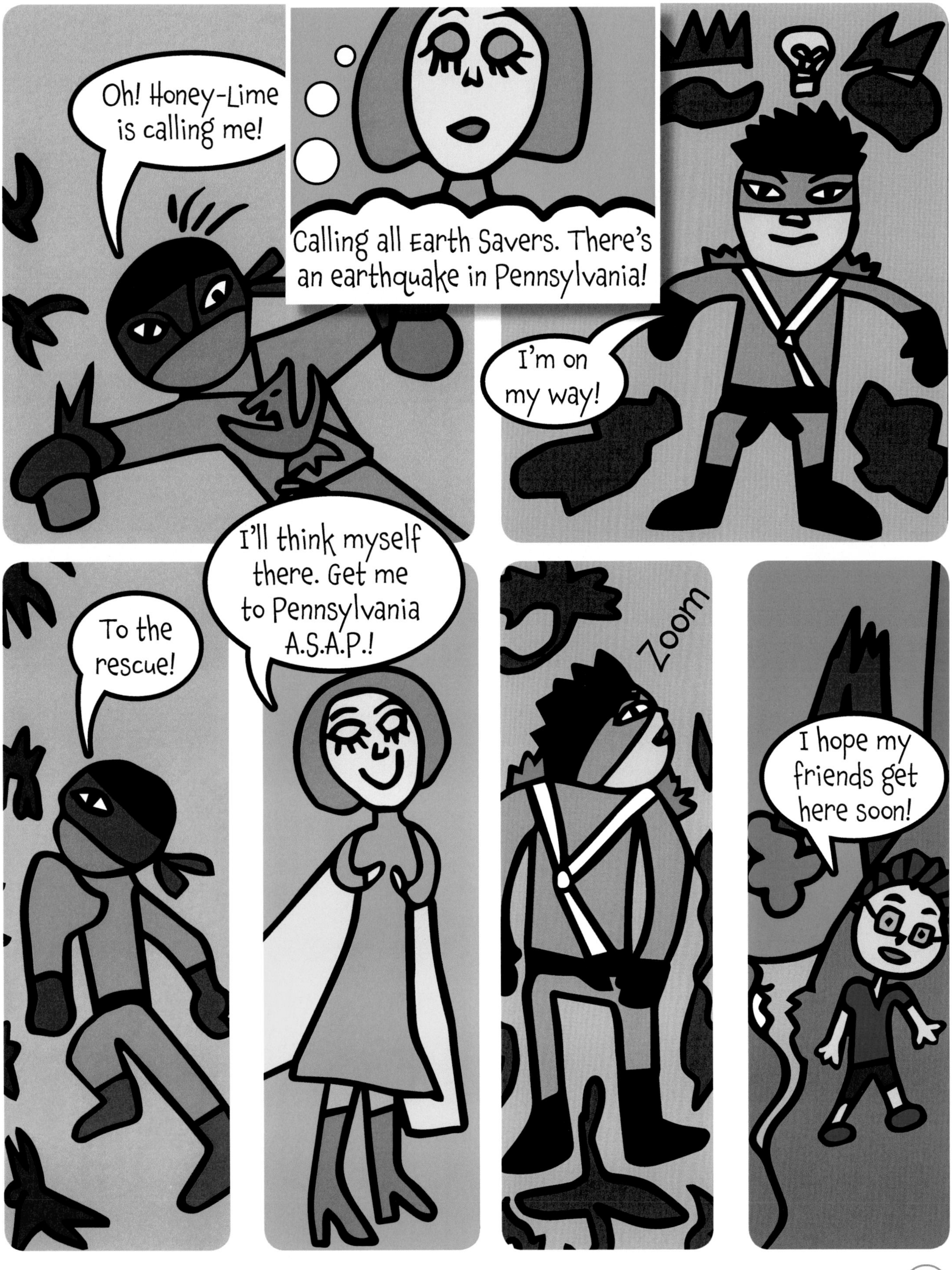
Oh! Honey-Lime is calling me!
Calling all Earth Savers. There's an earthquake in Pennsylvania!
I'm on my way!
To the rescue!
I'll think myself there. Get me to Pennsylvania A.S.A.P.!
Zoom
I hope my friends get here soon!

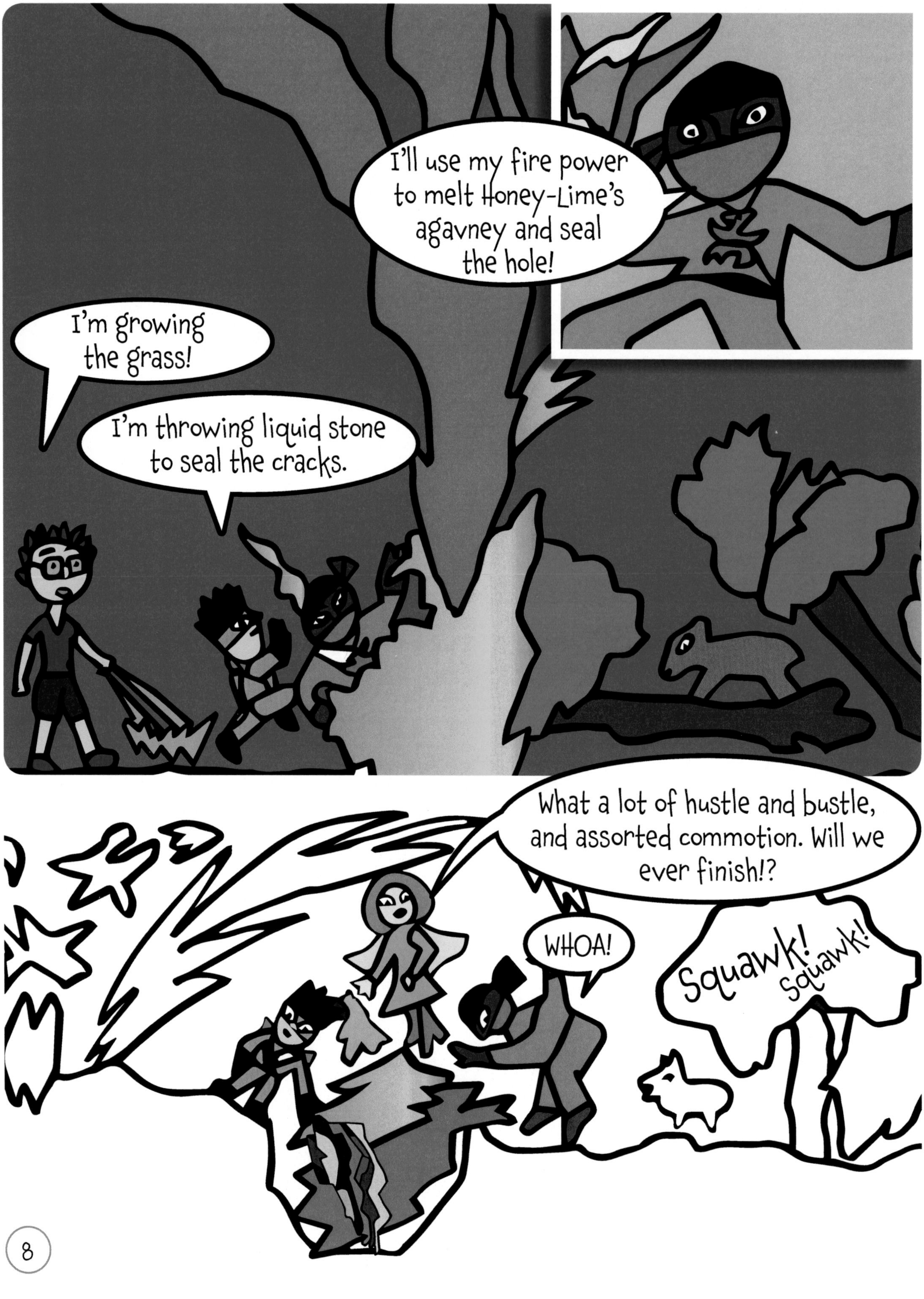
I'll use my fire power to melt Honey-Lime's agavney and seal the hole!
I'm growing the grass!
I'm throwing liquid stone to seal the cracks.
What a lot of hustle and bustle, and assorted commotion. Will we ever finish!?
WHOA!
Squawk! Squawk!

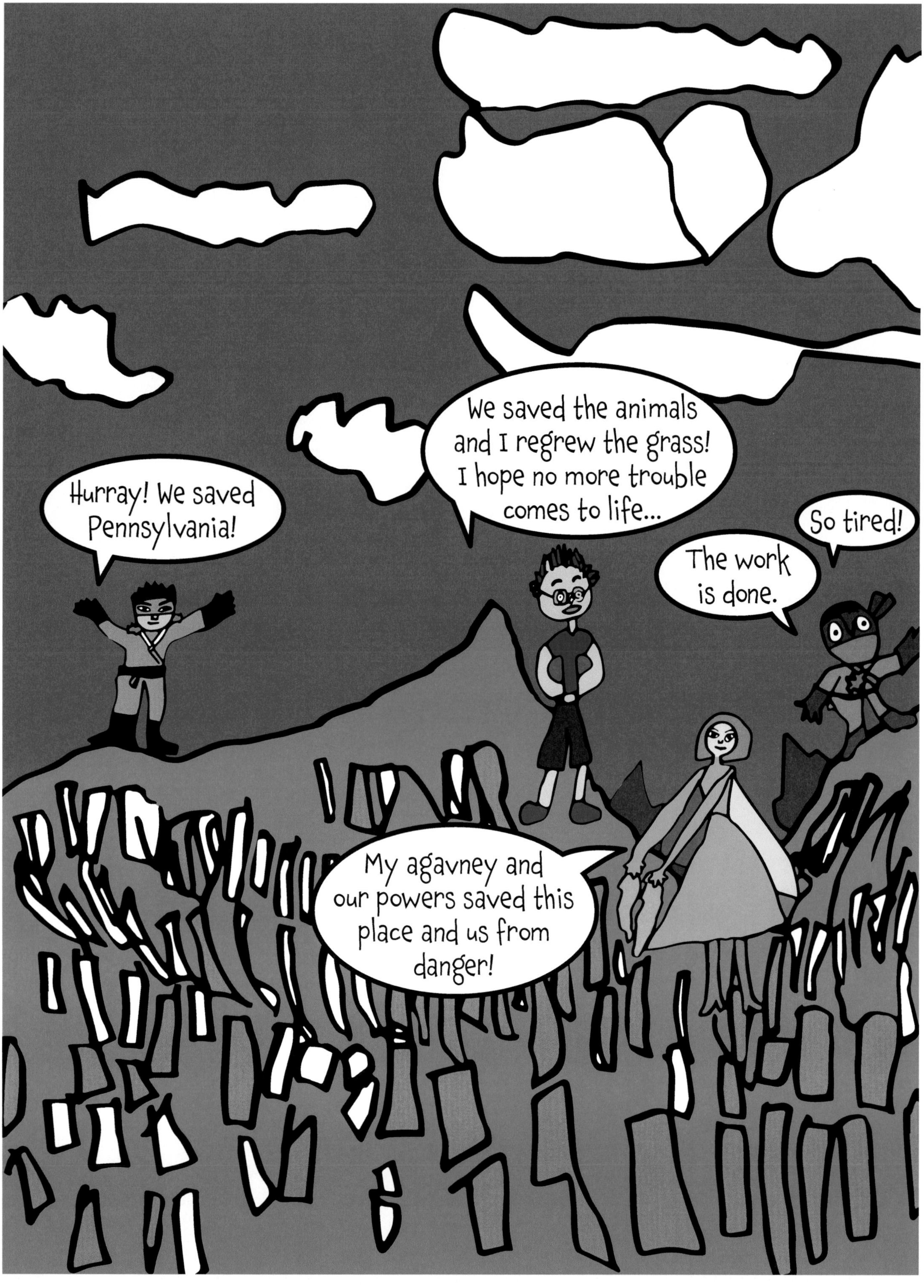
Hurray! We saved Pennsylvania!
We saved the animals and I regrew the grass! I hope no more trouble comes to life...
The work is done.
So tired!
My agavney and our powers saved this place and us from danger!

Chapter #2
The Message

In a galaxy far away...

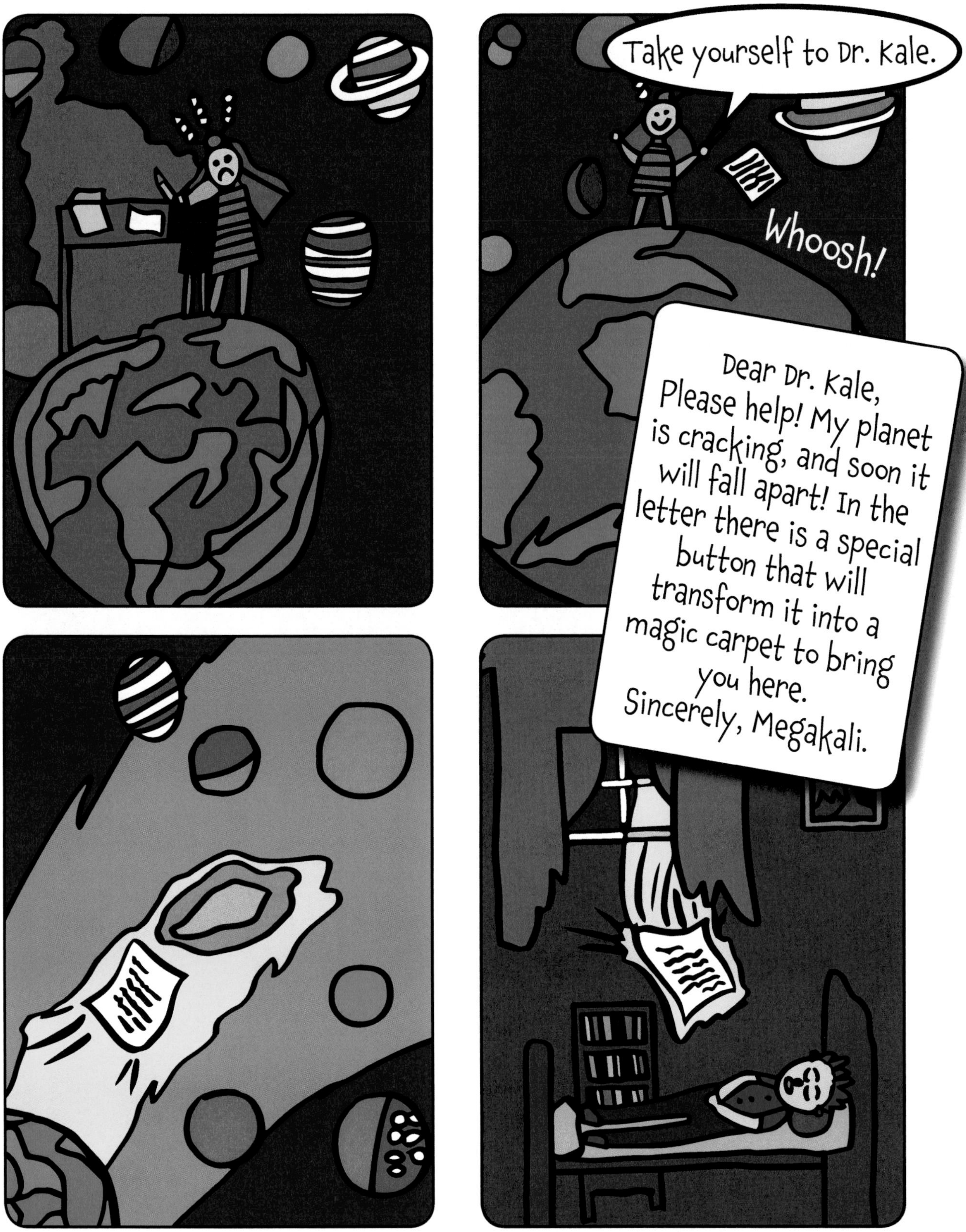
Take yourself to Dr. Kale.
Whoosh!
Dear Dr. Kale,
Please help! My planet is cracking, and soon it will fall apart! In the letter there is a special button that will transform it into a magic carpet to bring you here.
Sincerely, Megakali.

Dr. Kale is sleeping...

... and the letter slips through his window.

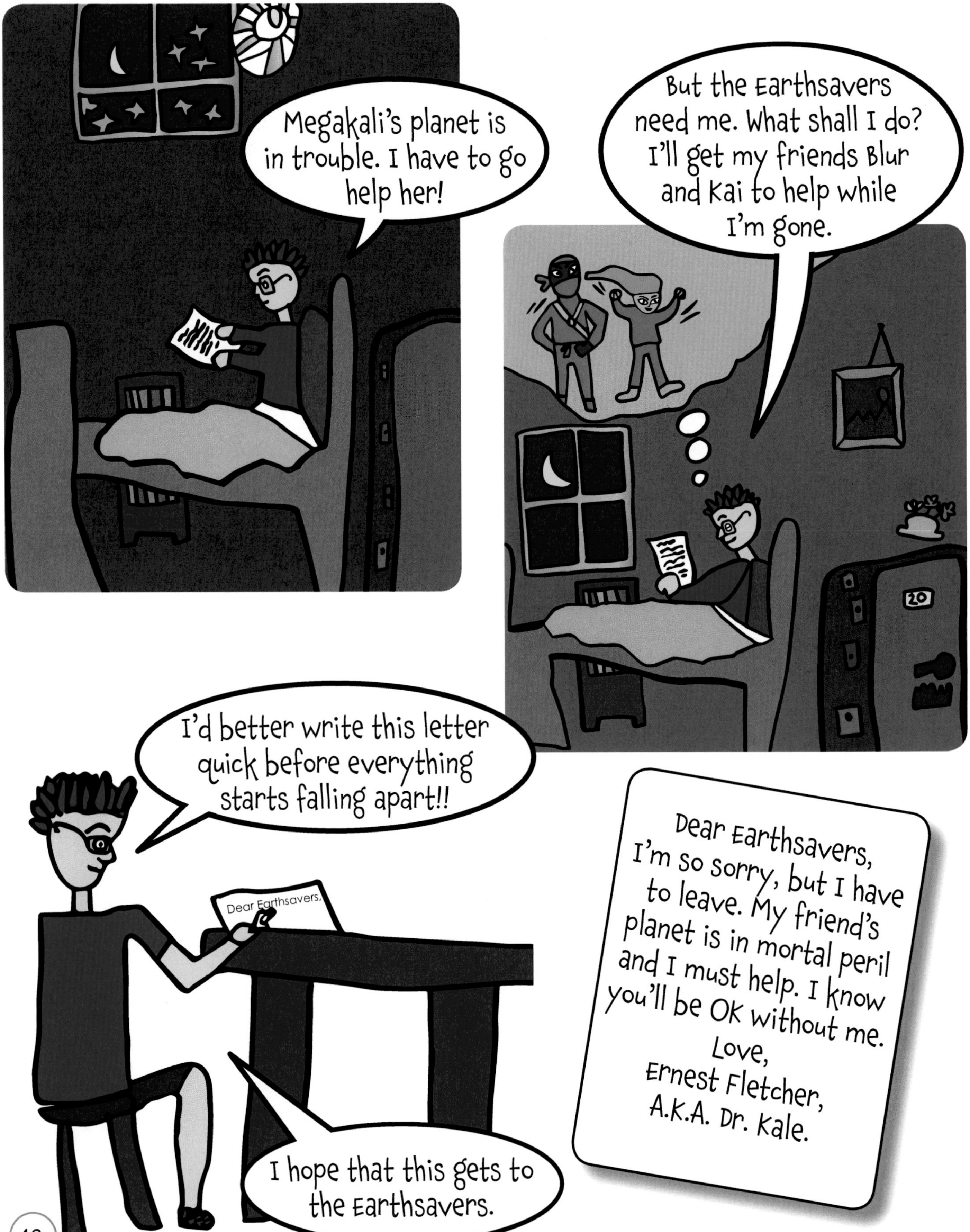

Megakali's planet is in trouble. I have to go help her!
But the Earthsavers need me. What shall I do? I'll get my friends Blur and Kai to help while I'm gone.
20
I'd better write this letter quick before everything starts falling apart!!
Dear Earthsavers,
I hope that this gets to the Earthsavers.
Dear Earthsavers,
I'm so sorry, but I have to leave. My friend's planet is in mortal peril and I must help. I know you'll be OK without me.
Love,
Ernest Fletcher,
A.K.A. Dr. Kale.

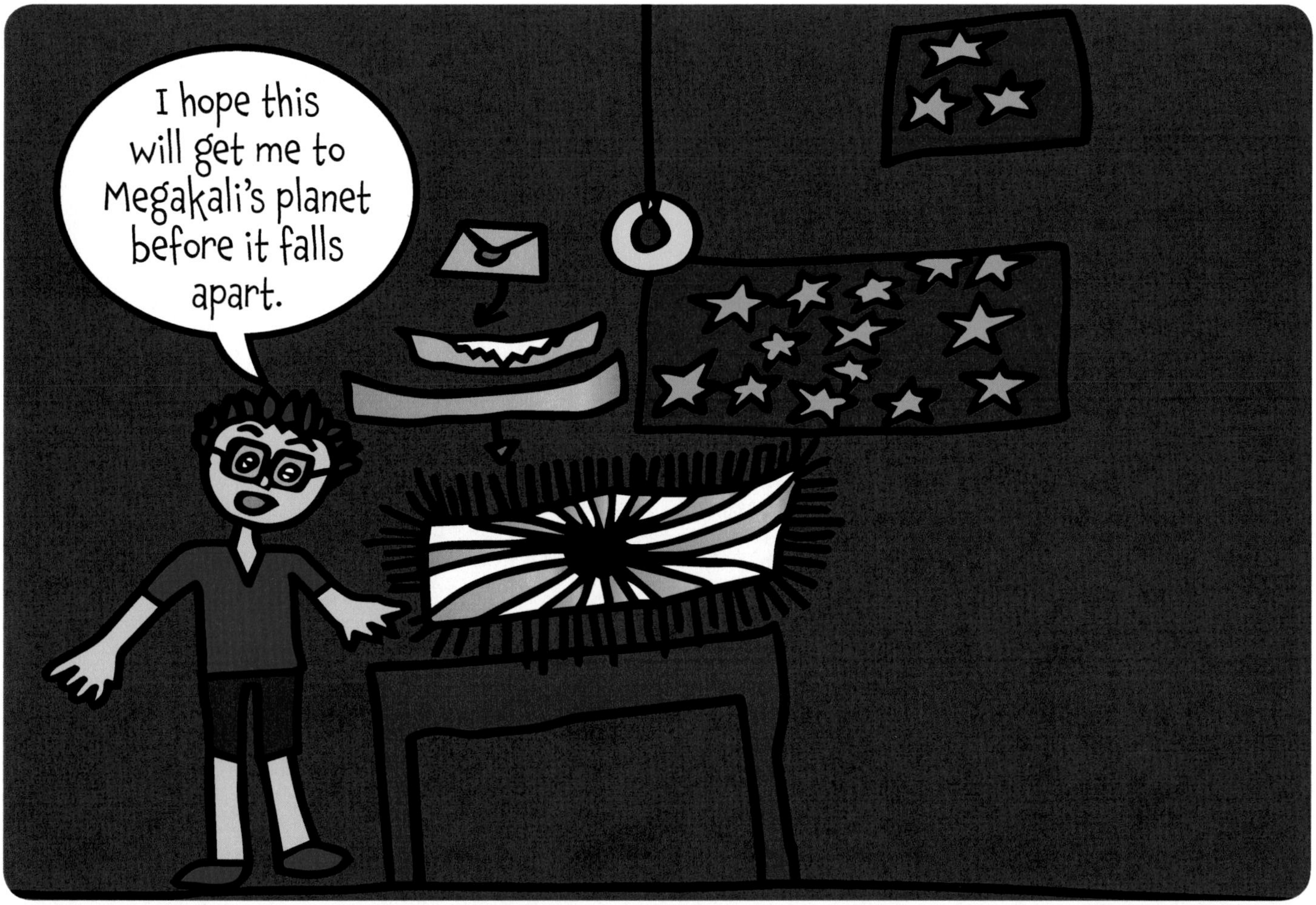
I hope this will get me to Megakali's planet before it falls apart.

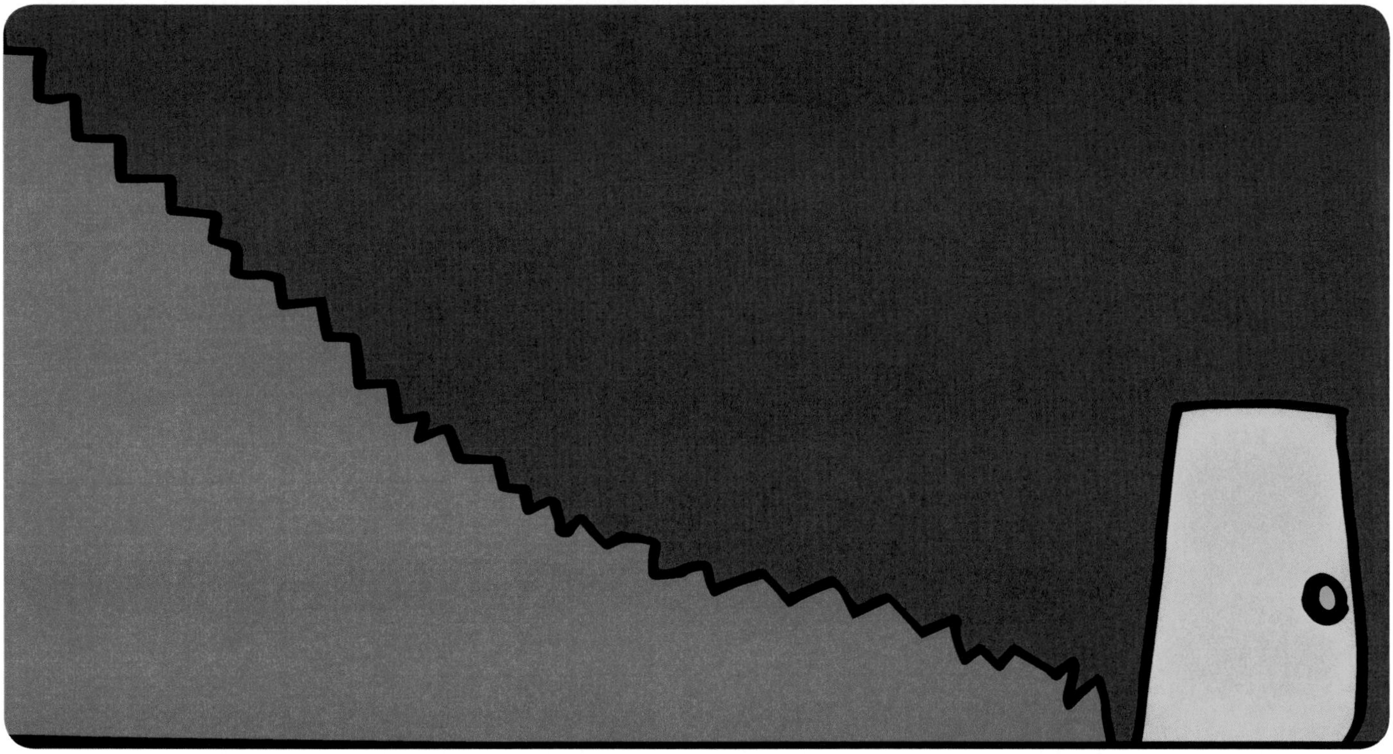

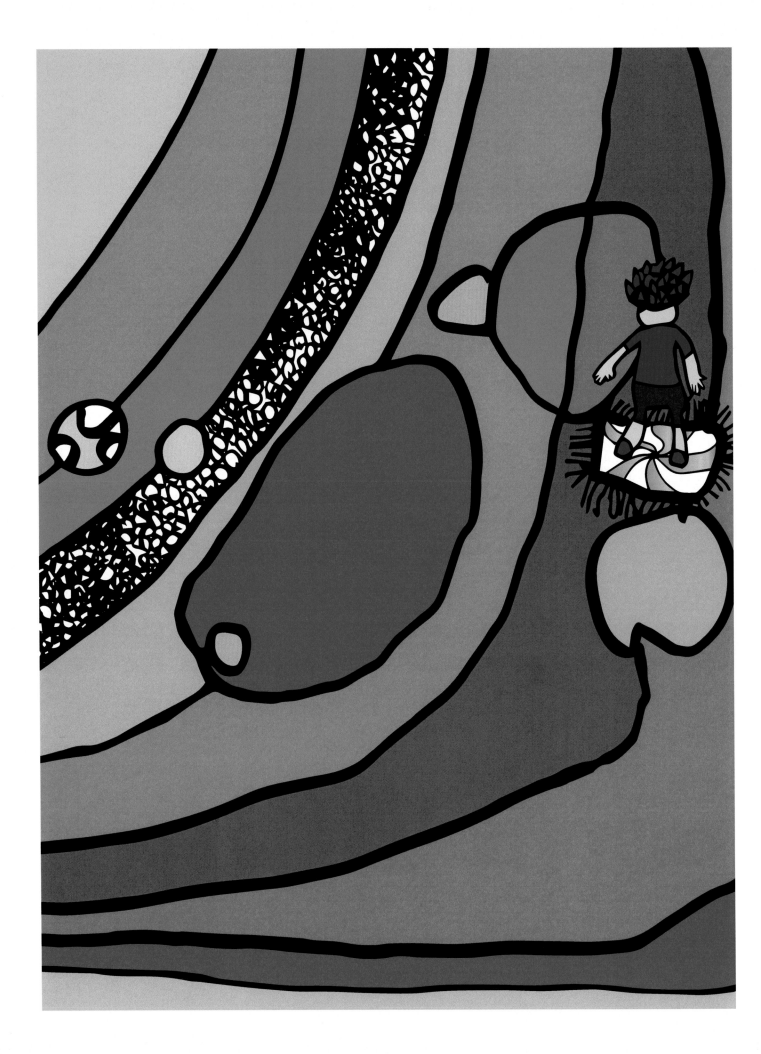

Chapter #3
The Earth Is Angry!

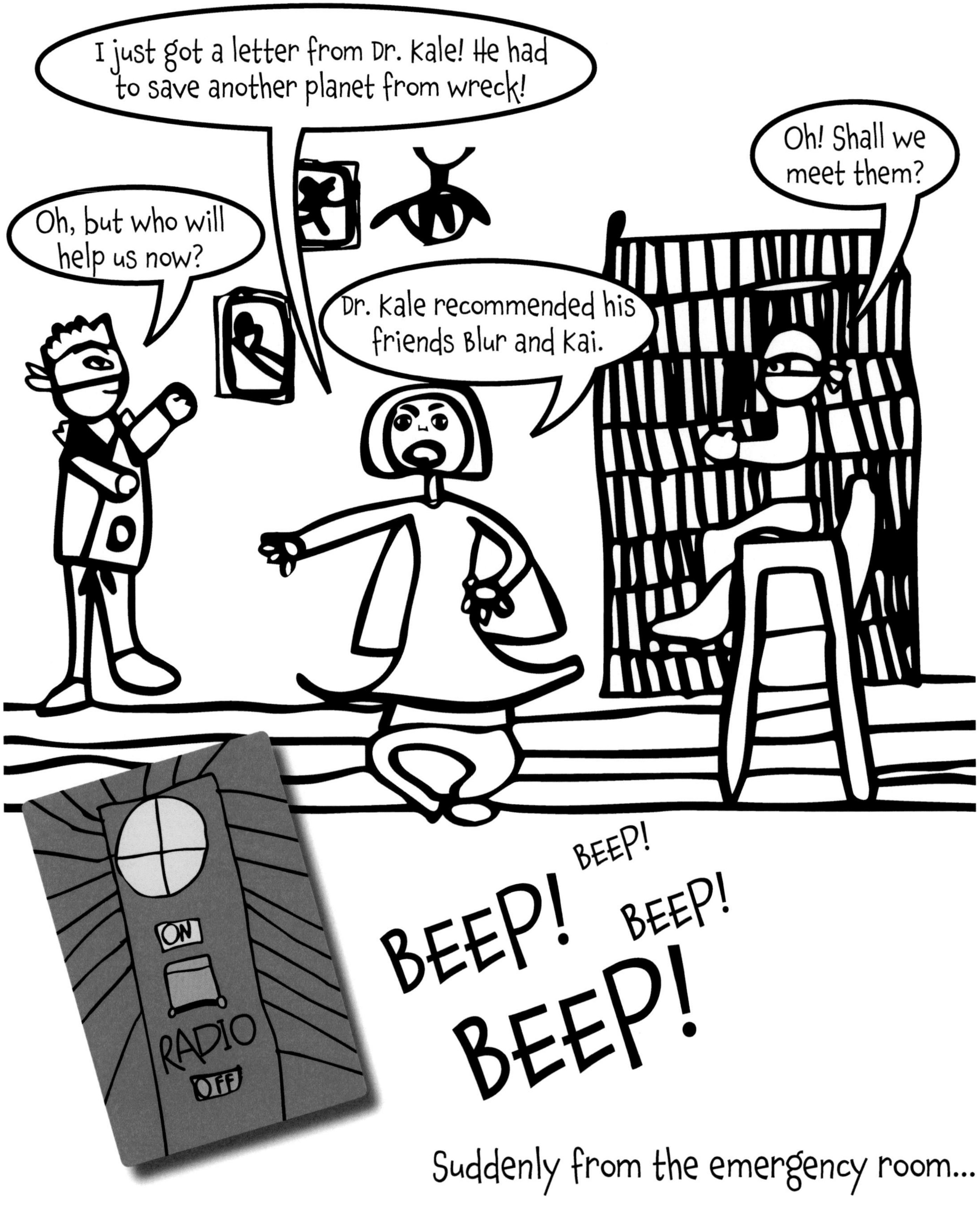
I just got a letter from Dr. Kale! He had to save another planet from wreck!
Oh, but who will help us now?
Dr. Kale recommended his friends Blur and Kai.
Oh! Shall we meet them?
ON
RADIO
OFF
BEEP!
BEEP!
BEEP!
BEEP!

Suddenly from the emergency room...

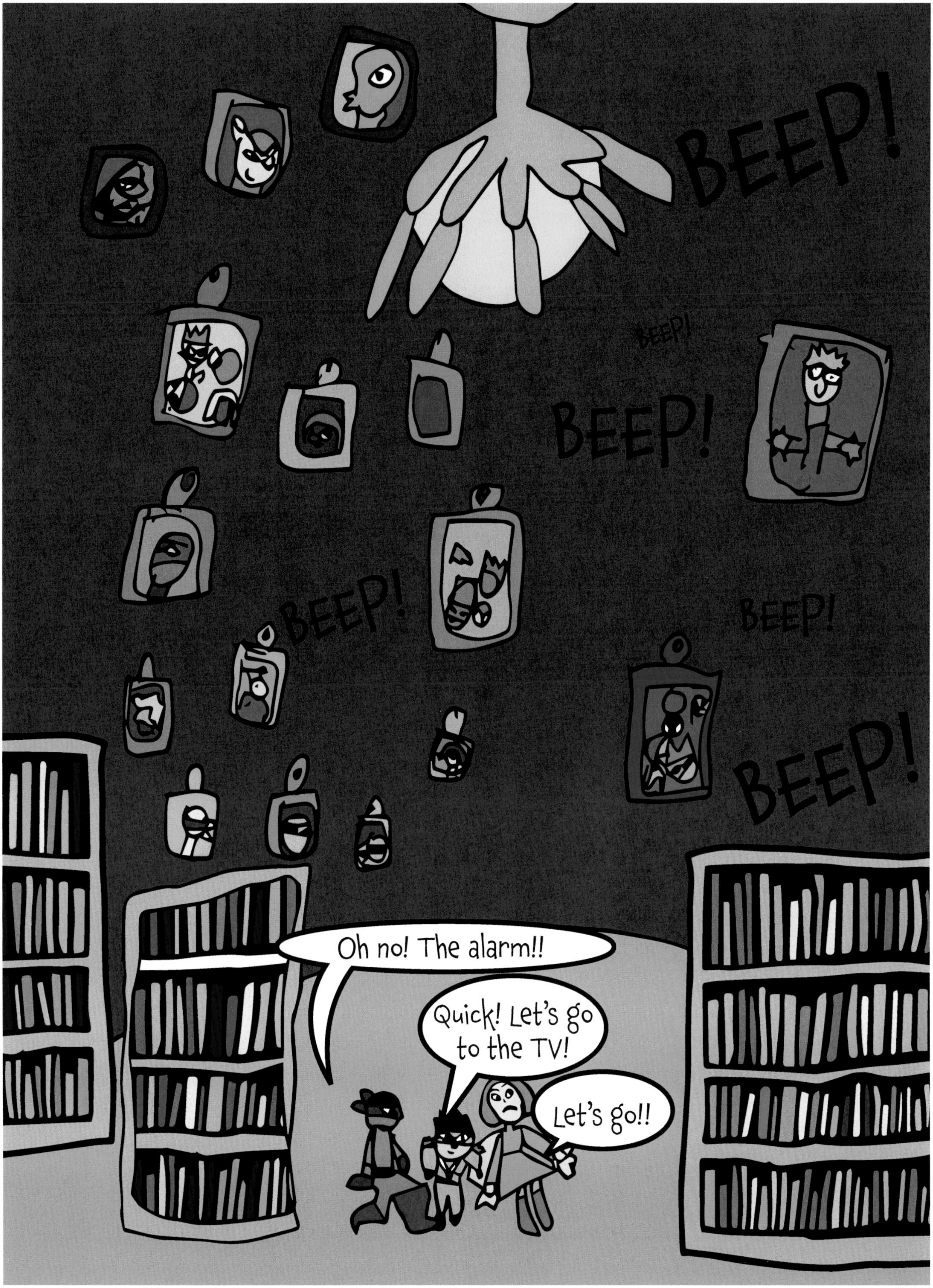
BEEP!
BEEP!
BEEP!
BEEP!
BEEP!
BEEP!
Oh no! The alarm!!
Quick! Let's go to the TV!
Let's go!!

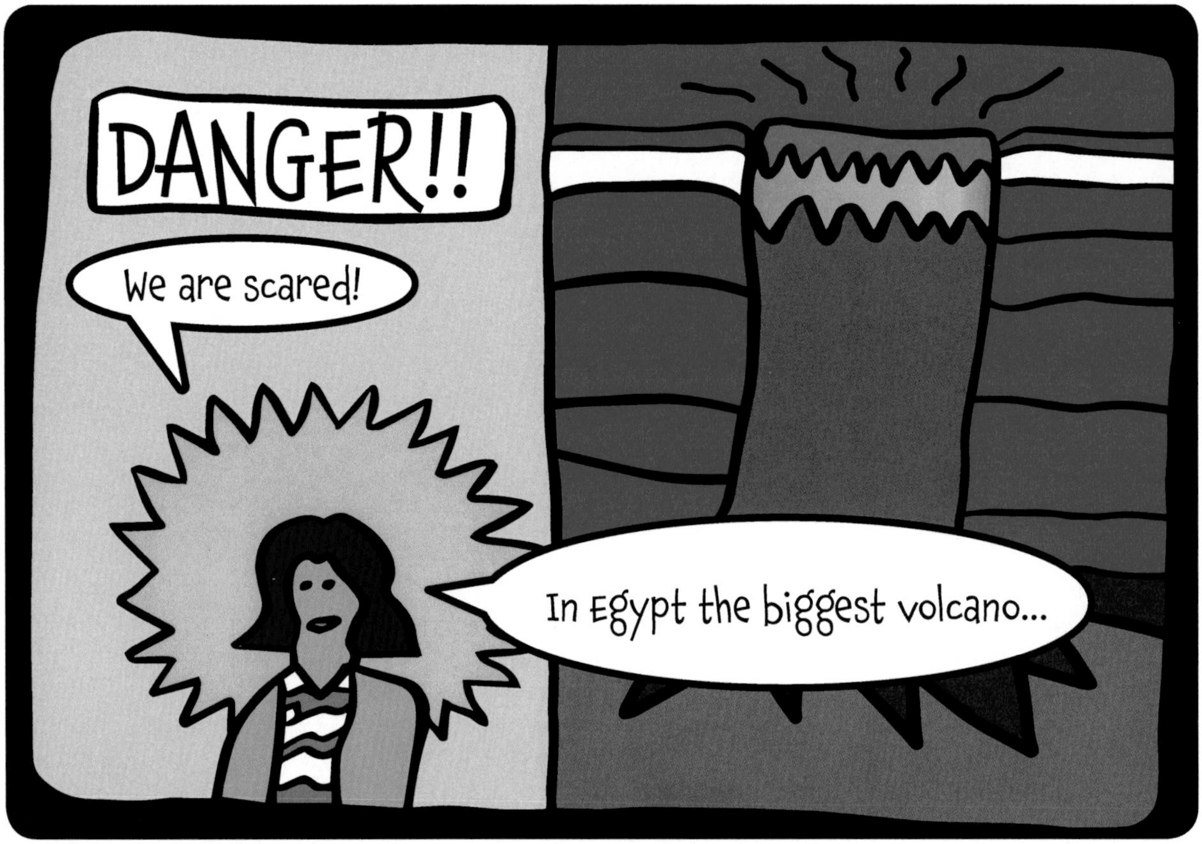
DANGER!!
We are scared!
In Egypt the biggest volcano...

On the news, the team sees a volcano erupting in Egypt!

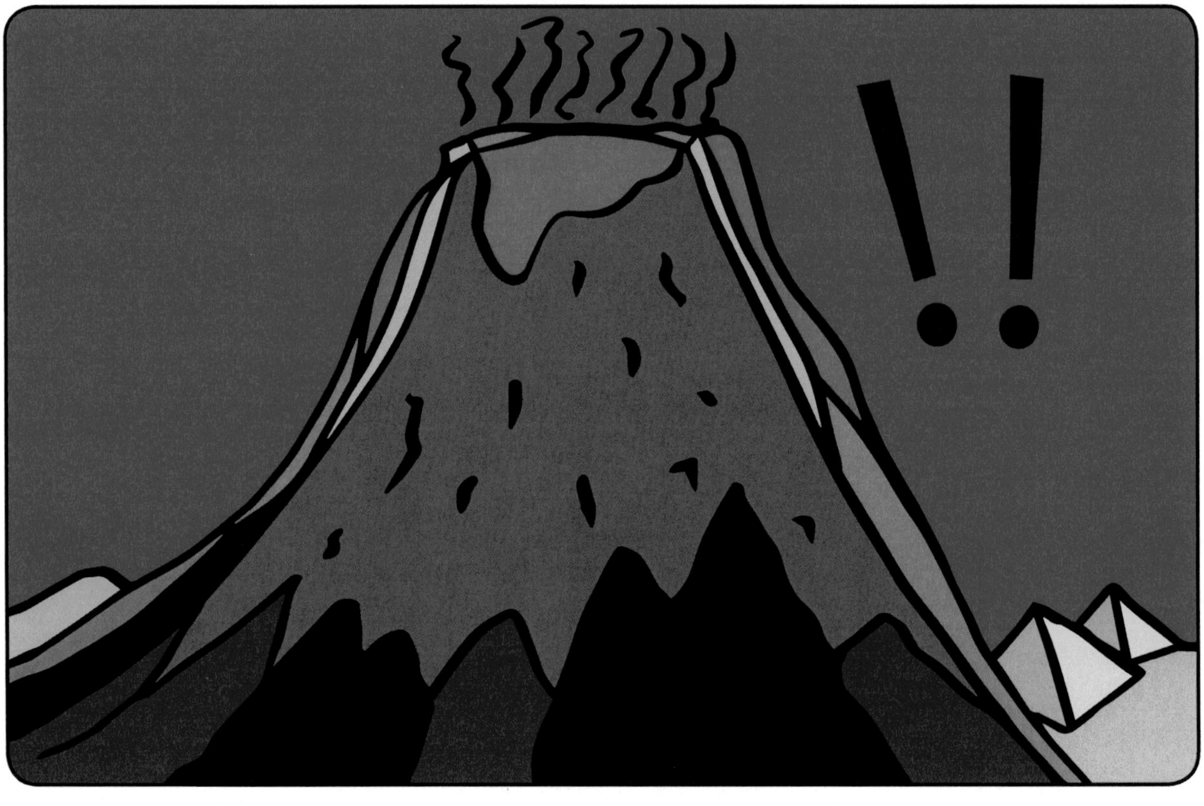
!!

Chapter #4
Farm Rescue

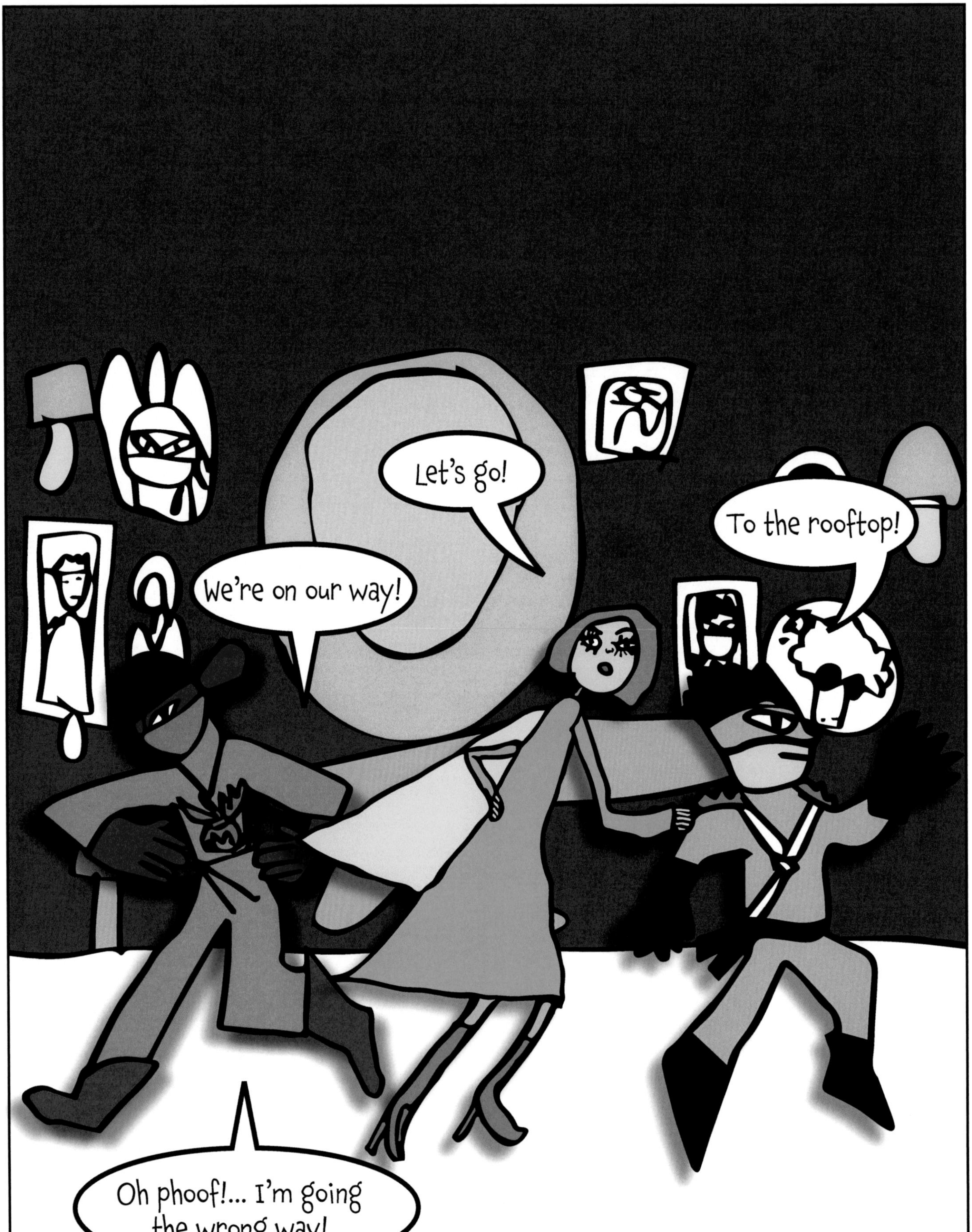
We're on our way!
Let's go!
To the rooftop!
Oh phoof!... I'm going the wrong way!

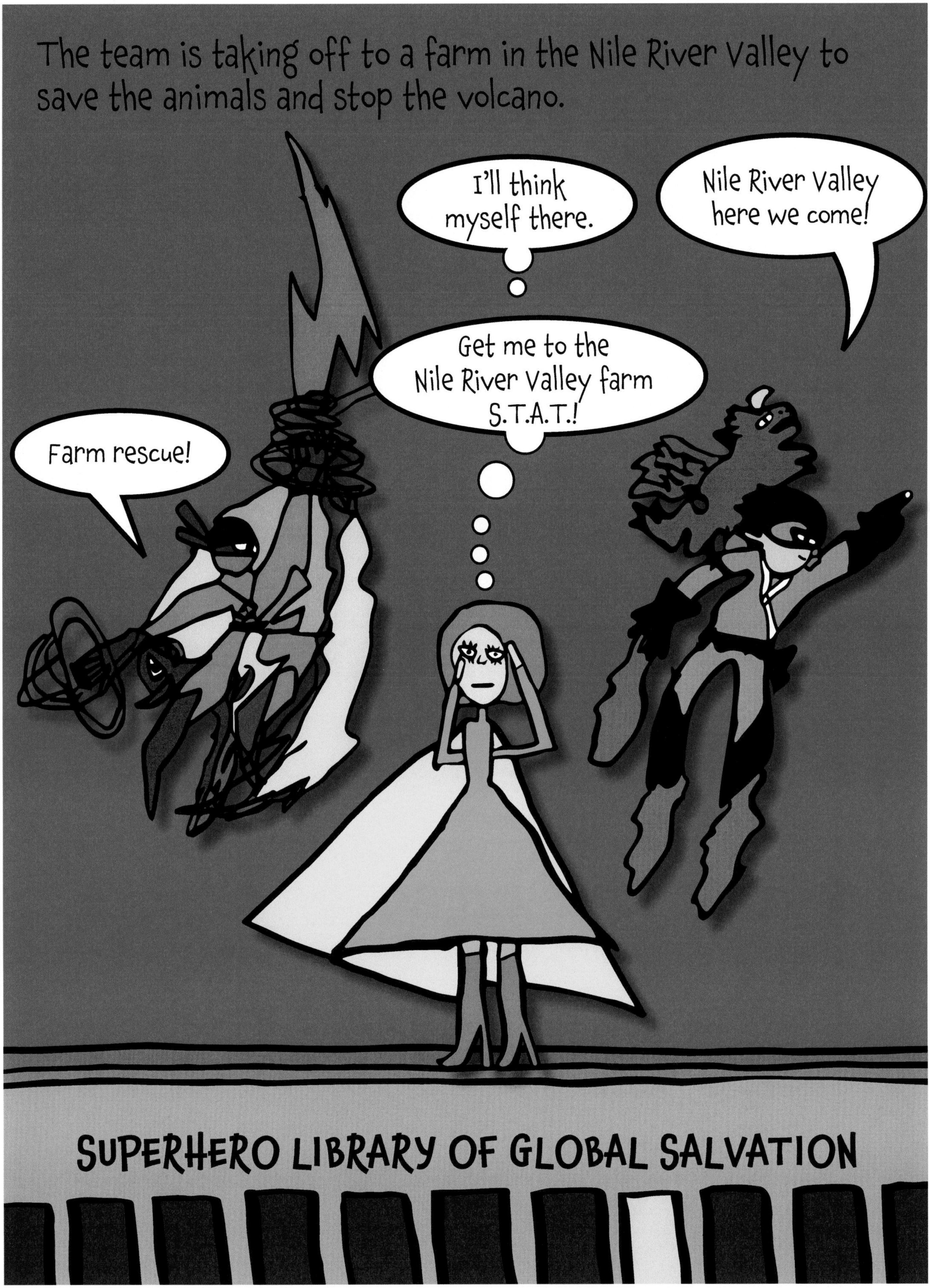
The team is taking off to a farm in the Nile River Valley to save the animals and stop the volcano.
I'll think myself there.
Nile River Valley here we come!
Get me to the Nile River Valley farm S.T.A.T.!
Farm rescue!
SUPERHERO LIBRARY OF GLOBAL SALVATION

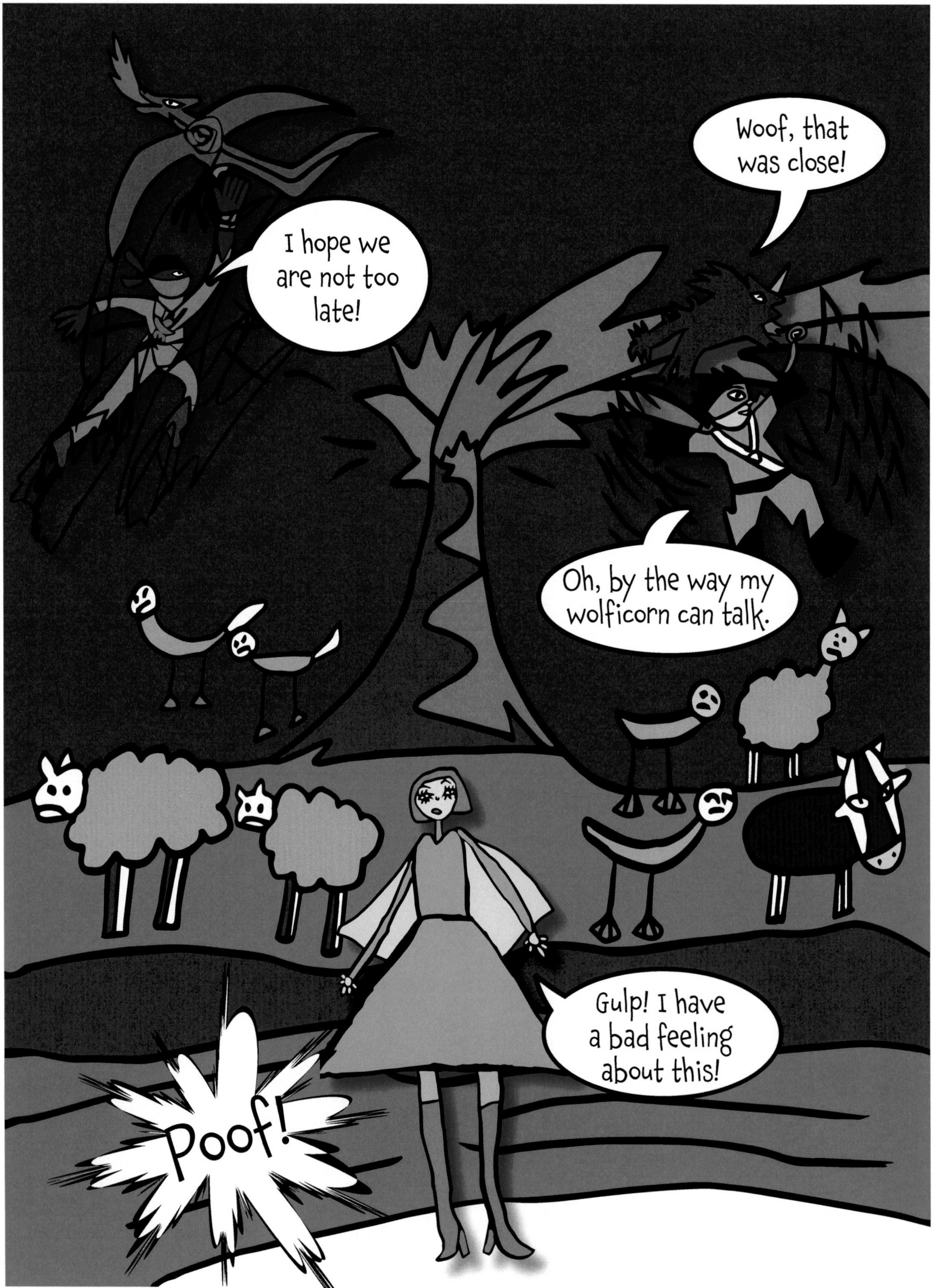
I hope we are not too late!
Woof, that was close!
Oh, by the way my wolficorn can talk.
Gulp! I have a bad feeling about this!
Poof!

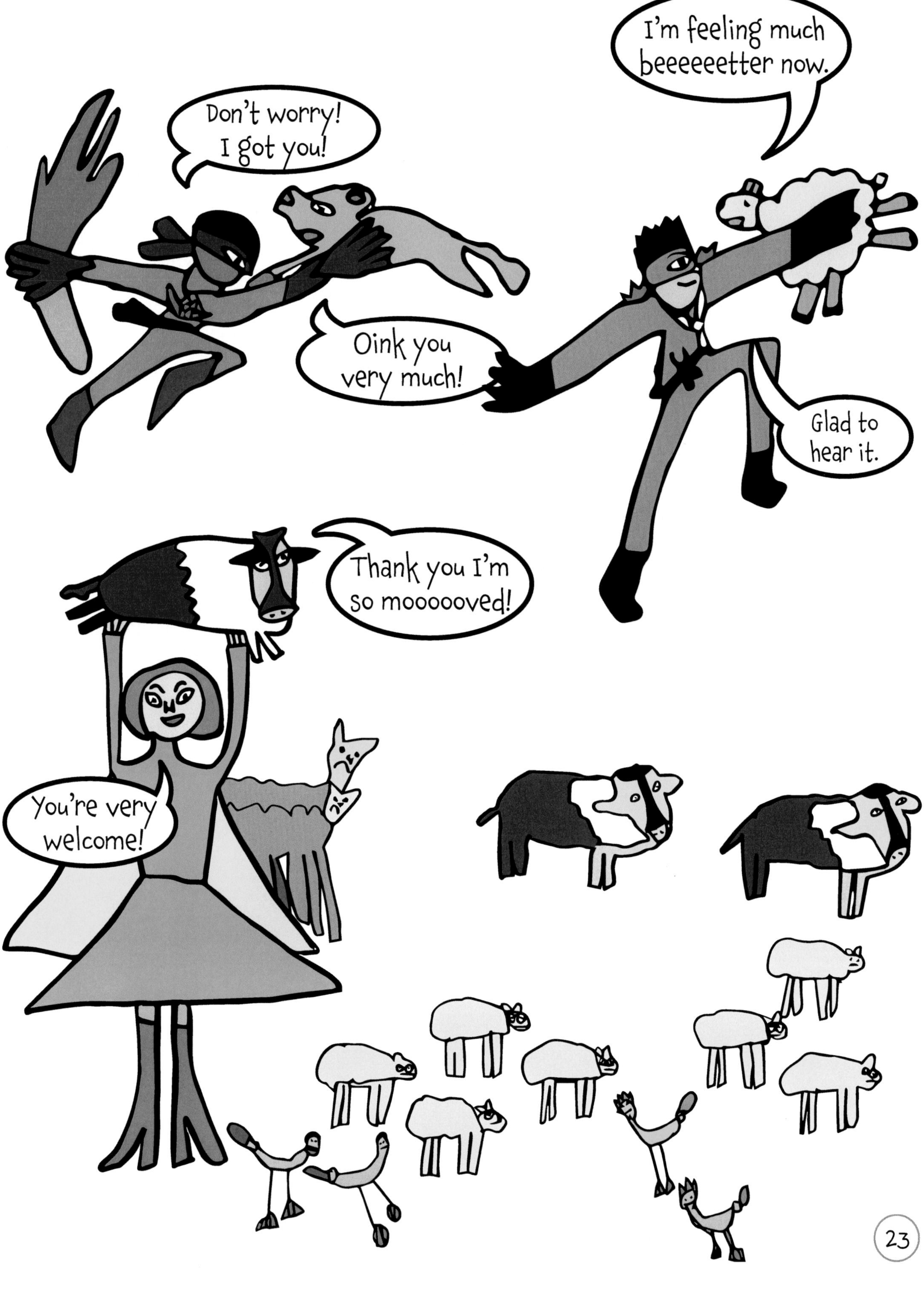
Don't worry! I got you!
I'm feeling much beeeeeetter now.
Oink you very much!
Glad to hear it.
Thank you I'm so moooooved!
You're very welcome!

Flame, Stone and Honey-Lime work together to stop the volcano! Stone cools the core and Honey-Lime fills holes with agavney. Flame melts Honey-Lime's agavney to seal the cracks.

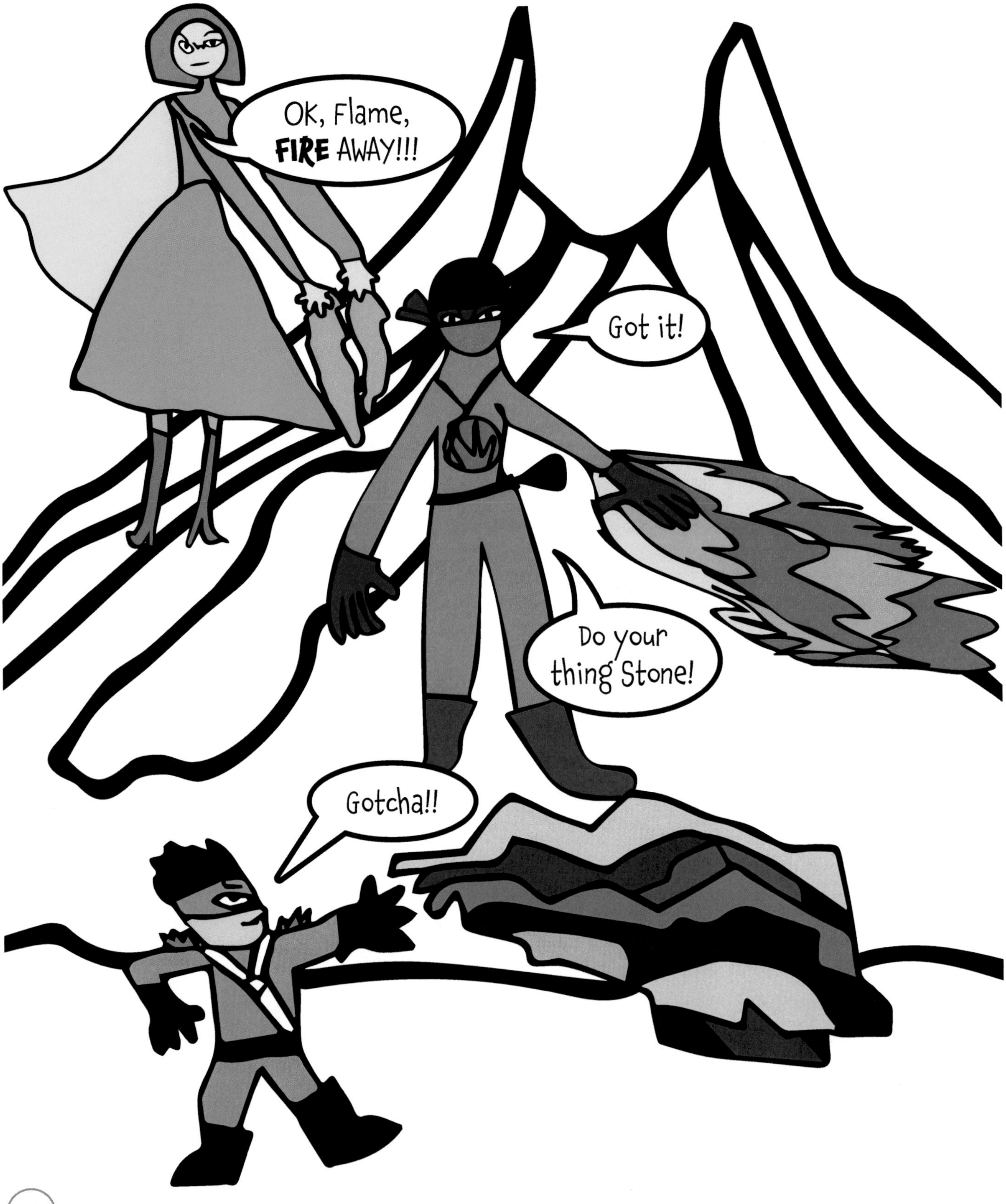
OK, Flame, **FIRE** AWAY!!!
Got it!
Do your thing Stone!
Gotcha!!

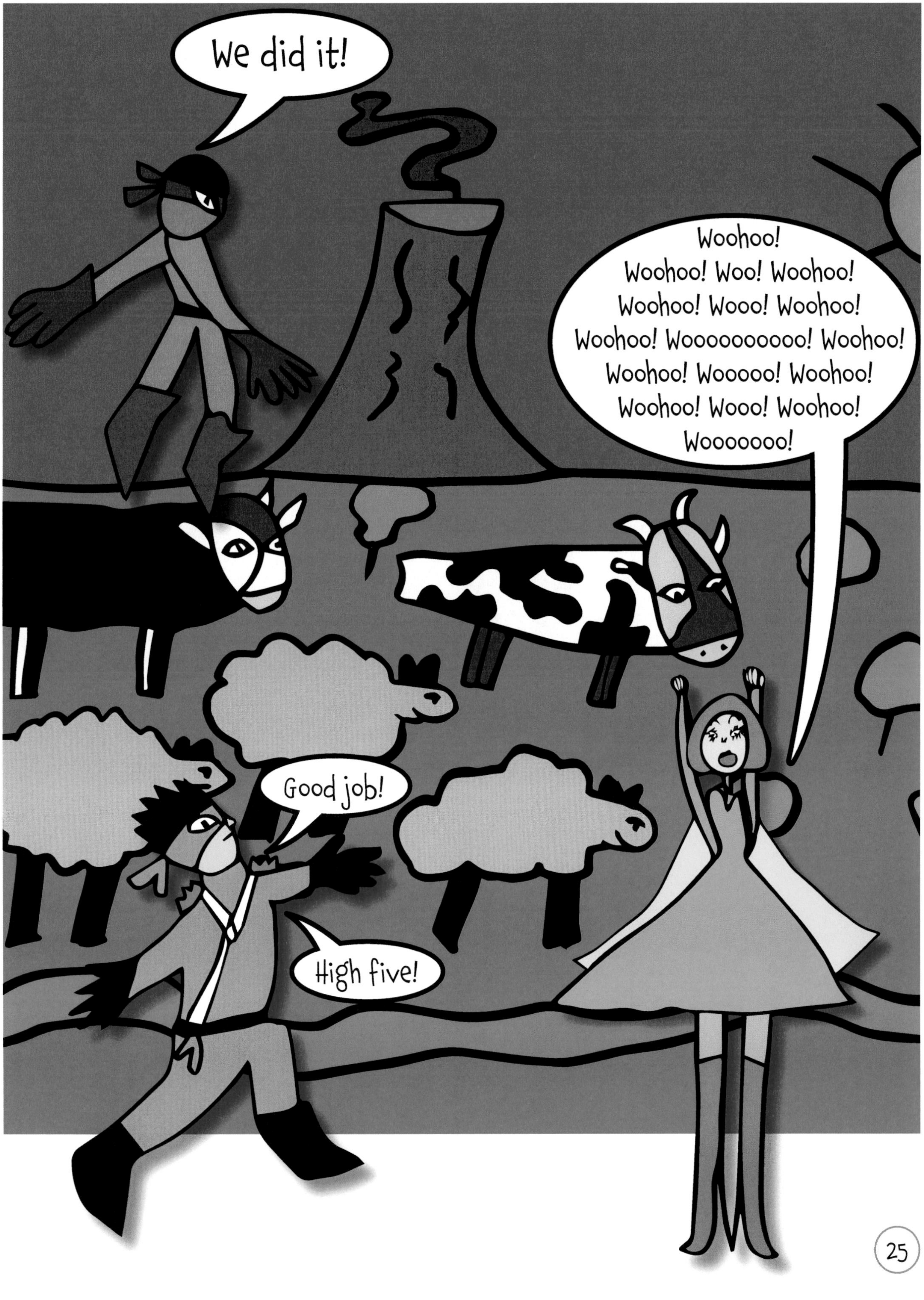
We did it!
Woohoo! Woohoo! Woo! Woohoo! Woohoo! Wooo! Woohoo! Woohoo! Woooooooooo! Woohoo! Woohoo! Wooooo! Woohoo! Woohoo! Wooo! Woohoo! Wooooooo!
Good job!
High five!

Chapter #5
The New Heroes

Kai's underwater fake volcano home.

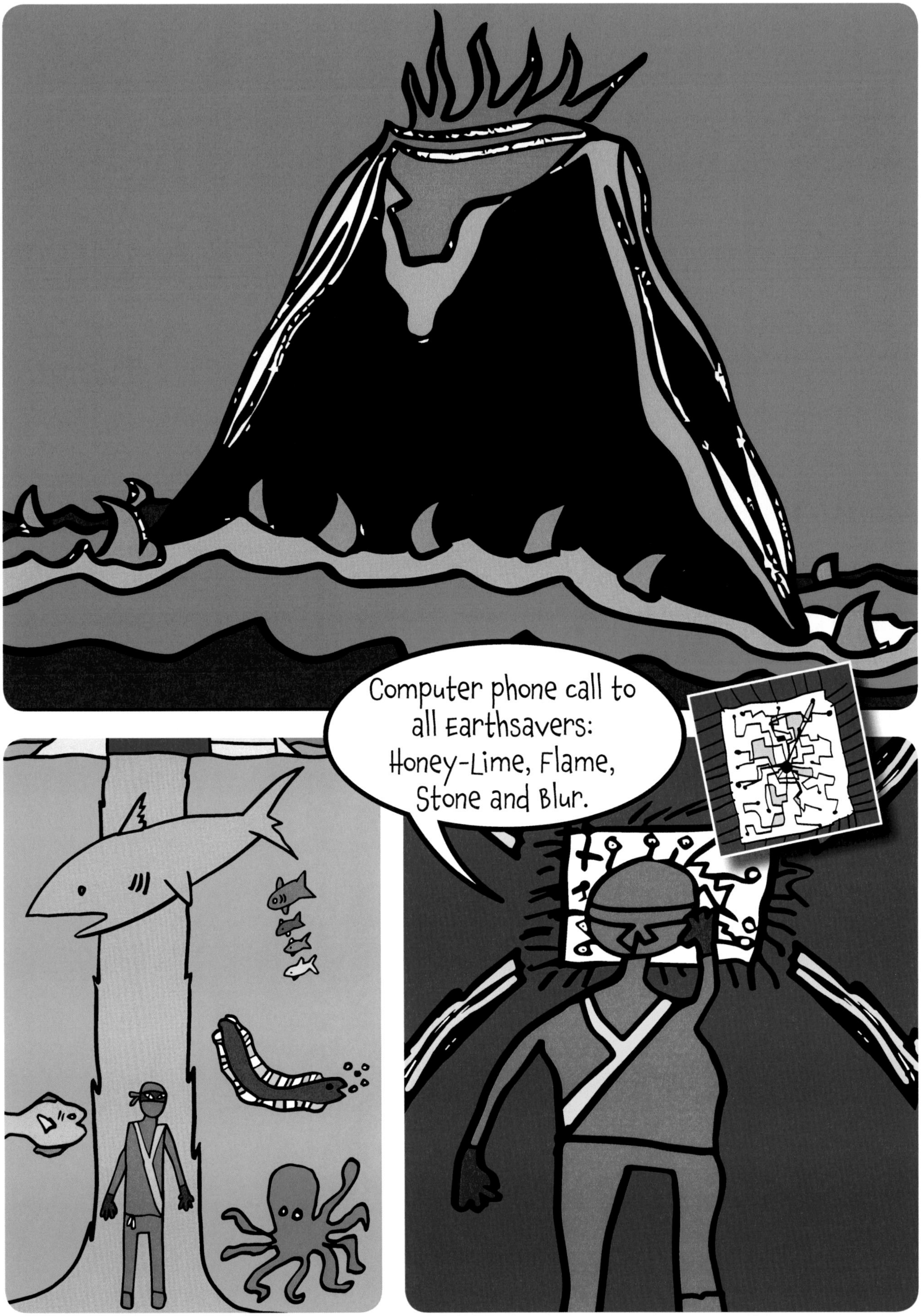
Computer phone call to all Earthsavers: Honey-Lime, Flame, Stone and Blur.

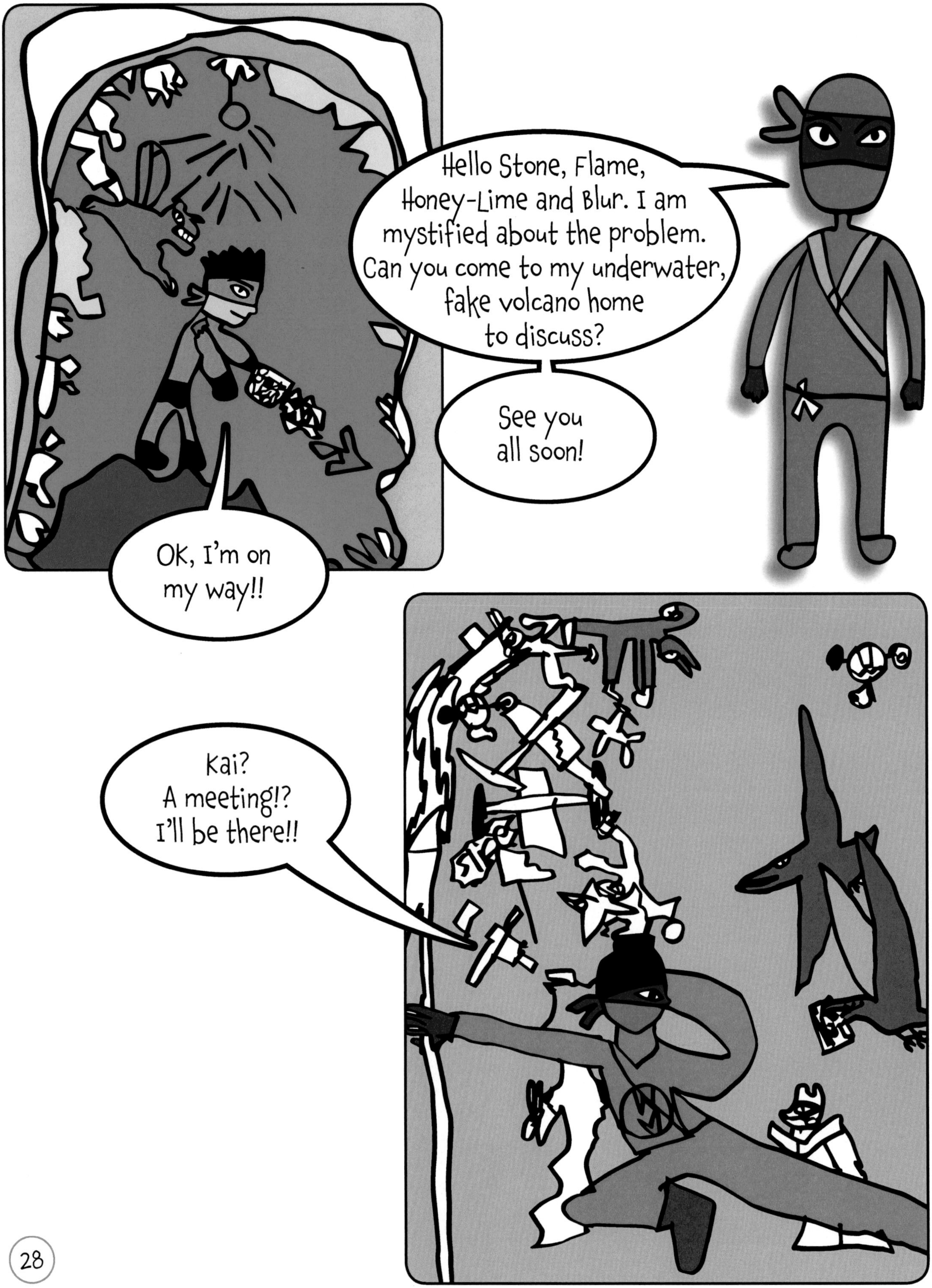
Hello Stone, Flame, Honey-Lime and Blur. I am mystified about the problem. Can you come to my underwater, fake volcano home to discuss?
See you all soon!
OK, I'm on my way!!
Kai? A meeting!? I'll be there!!

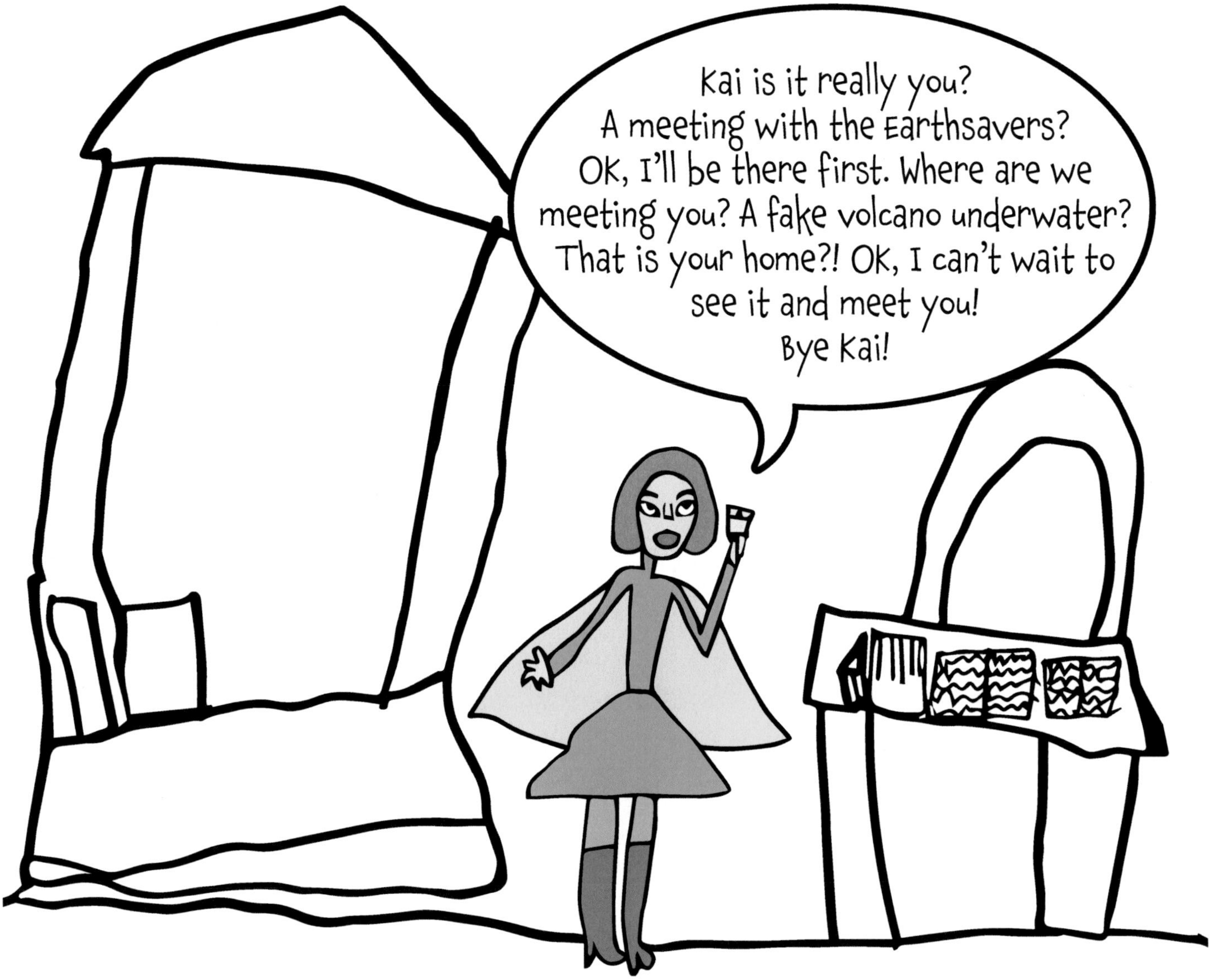
Kai is it really you?
A meeting with the Earthsavers?
OK, I'll be there first. Where are we
meeting you? A fake volcano underwater?
That is your home?! OK, I can't wait to
see it and meet you!
Bye Kai!

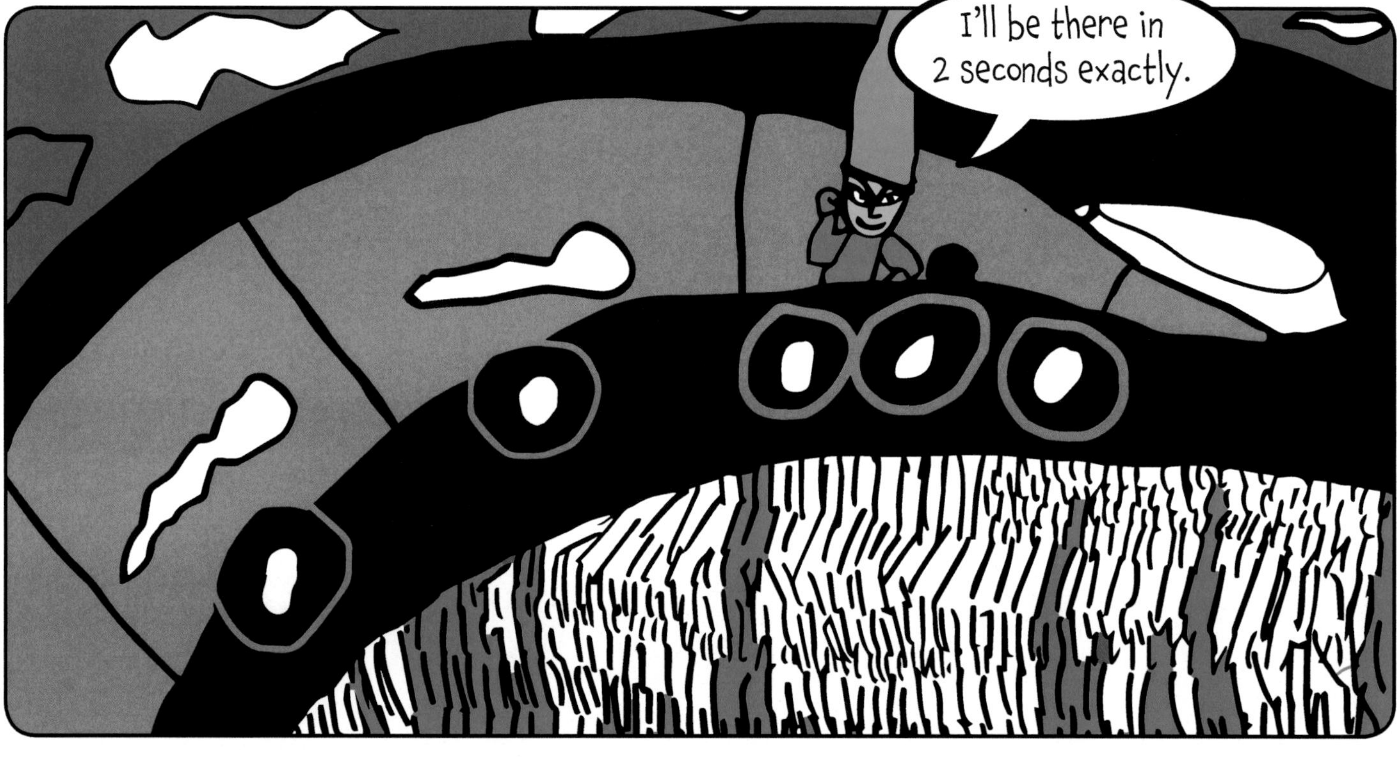
I'll be there in
2 seconds exactly.

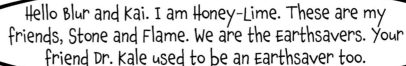 Hello Blur and Kai. I am Honey-Lime. These are my friends, Stone and Flame. We are the Earthsavers. Your friend Dr. Kale used to be an Earthsaver too.

Hello Earthsavers, my name is Blur! So what's the problem?

Hi everyone, I'm Kai.

 Here's the problem. Massive earthquakes are happening all over the world. In fact we just escaped a volcano, which to me, is involved with this earthquake business. Even though earthquakes that happen, maybe daily, are too small to feel, these ones are different and can destroy the entire world. We need to help!

 My superpowers are: one lung and one gill which allows me to breathe on land and in water. I also meditate to calm anything down. How can I help you guys with the problem?

 Great Kai. You can balance the Earth's core so there are no earthquakes underwater or on land.

Ok! Now I know how to help!

I have super strength and can run lightning fast. How can I help?

 Ok, great! You can run from spot to spot and hold the ground so it stops quaking.

 OK, sure.

 OK, so we have a plan! We'll be ready for the next one.

Chapter #6
Cracking The Code

Meanwhile, back at the Superhero Library of Global Salvation, Honey-Lime is searching for the right book!

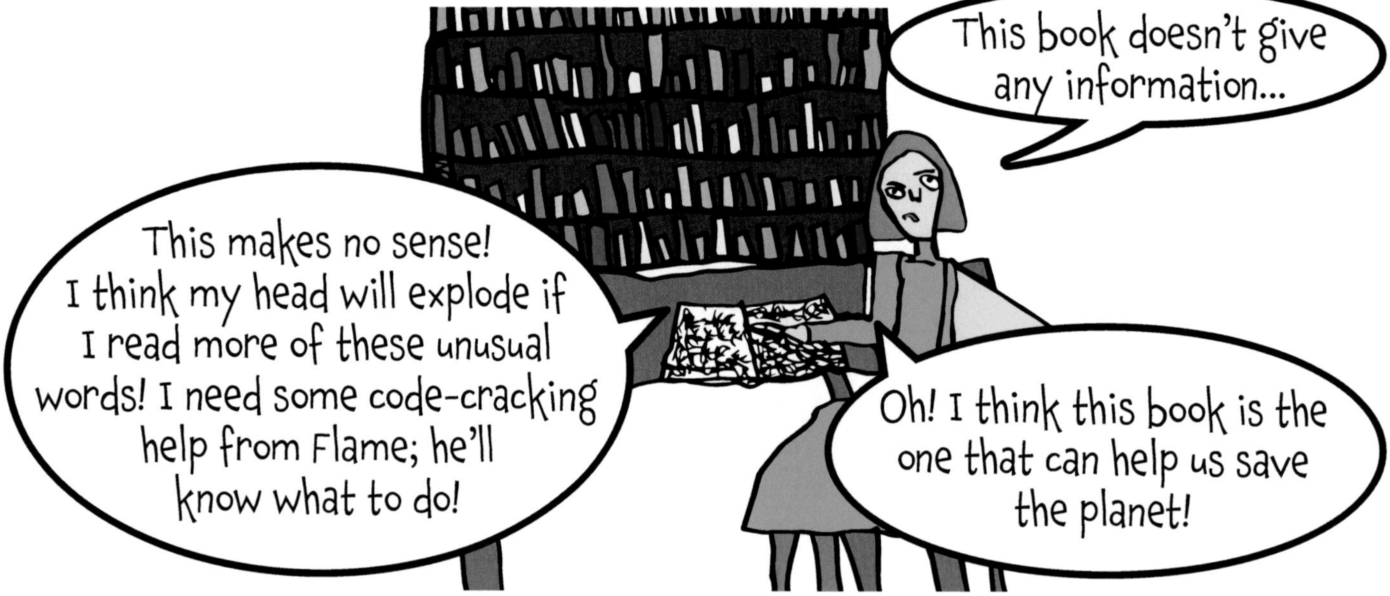
This book doesn't give any information...
This makes no sense! I think my head will explode if I read more of these unusual words! I need some code-cracking help from Flame; he'll know what to do!
Oh! I think this book is the one that can help us save the planet!

Honey-Lime runs out in desperation searching for Flame...

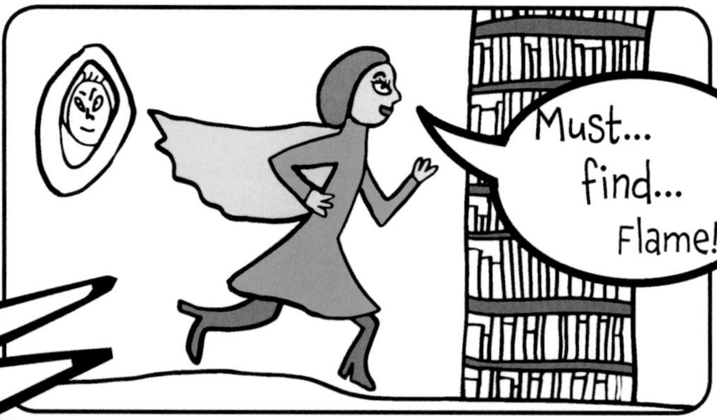
Must... find... Flame!

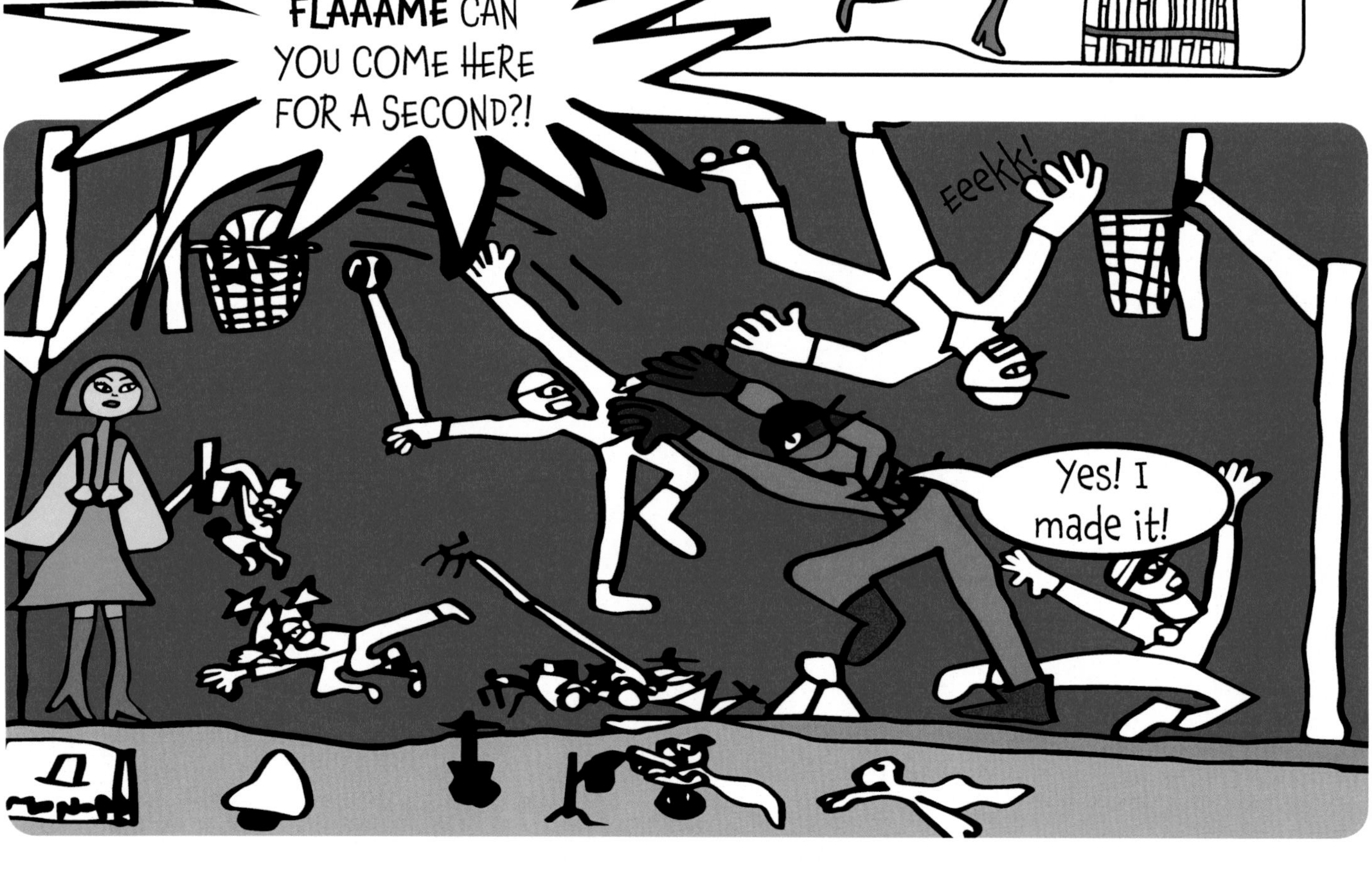
FLAAAME CAN YOU COME HERE FOR A SECOND?!
Eeekk!
Yes! I made it!

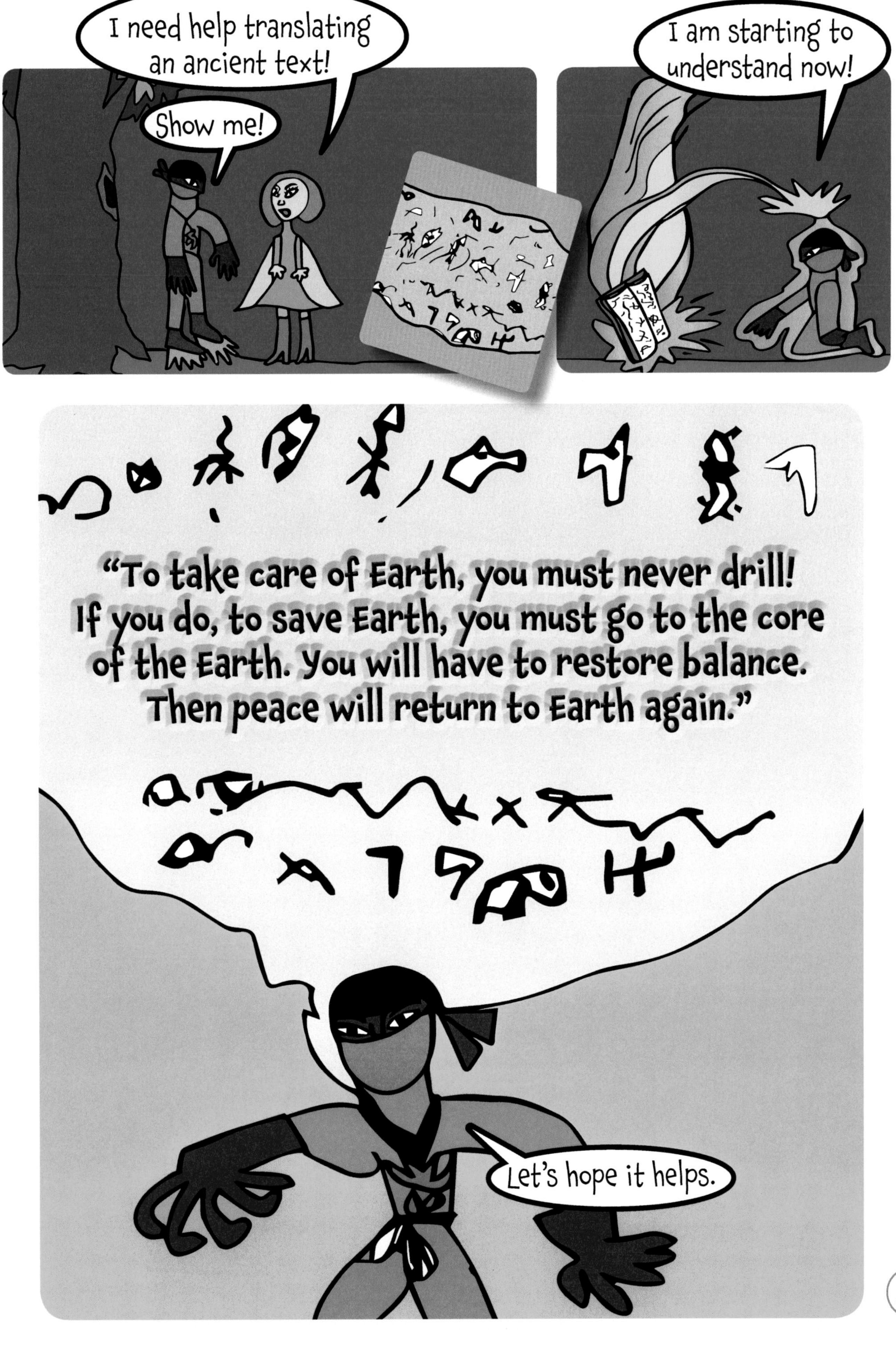
I need help translating an ancient text!
Show me!
I am starting to understand now!
"To take care of Earth, you must never drill! If you do, to save Earth, you must go to the core of the Earth. You will have to restore balance. Then peace will return to Earth again."
Let's hope it helps.

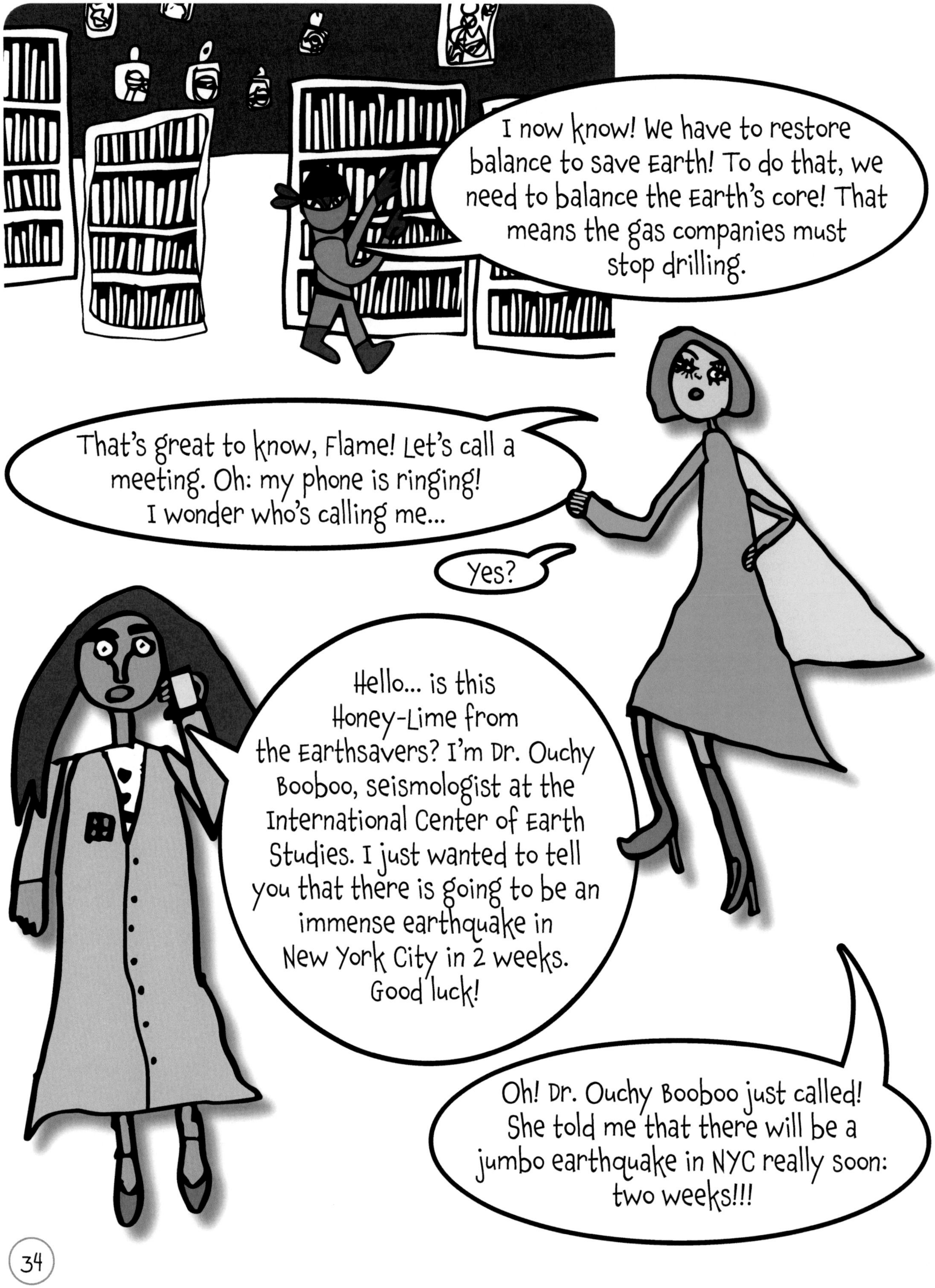
I now know! We have to restore balance to save Earth! To do that, we need to balance the Earth's core! That means the gas companies must stop drilling.
That's great to know, Flame! Let's call a meeting. Oh: my phone is ringing! I wonder who's calling me...
Yes?
Hello... is this Honey-Lime from the Earthsavers? I'm Dr. Ouchy Booboo, seismologist at the International Center of Earth Studies. I just wanted to tell you that there is going to be an immense earthquake in New York City in 2 weeks. Good luck!
Oh! Dr. Ouchy Booboo just called! She told me that there will be a jumbo earthquake in NYC really soon: two weeks!!!

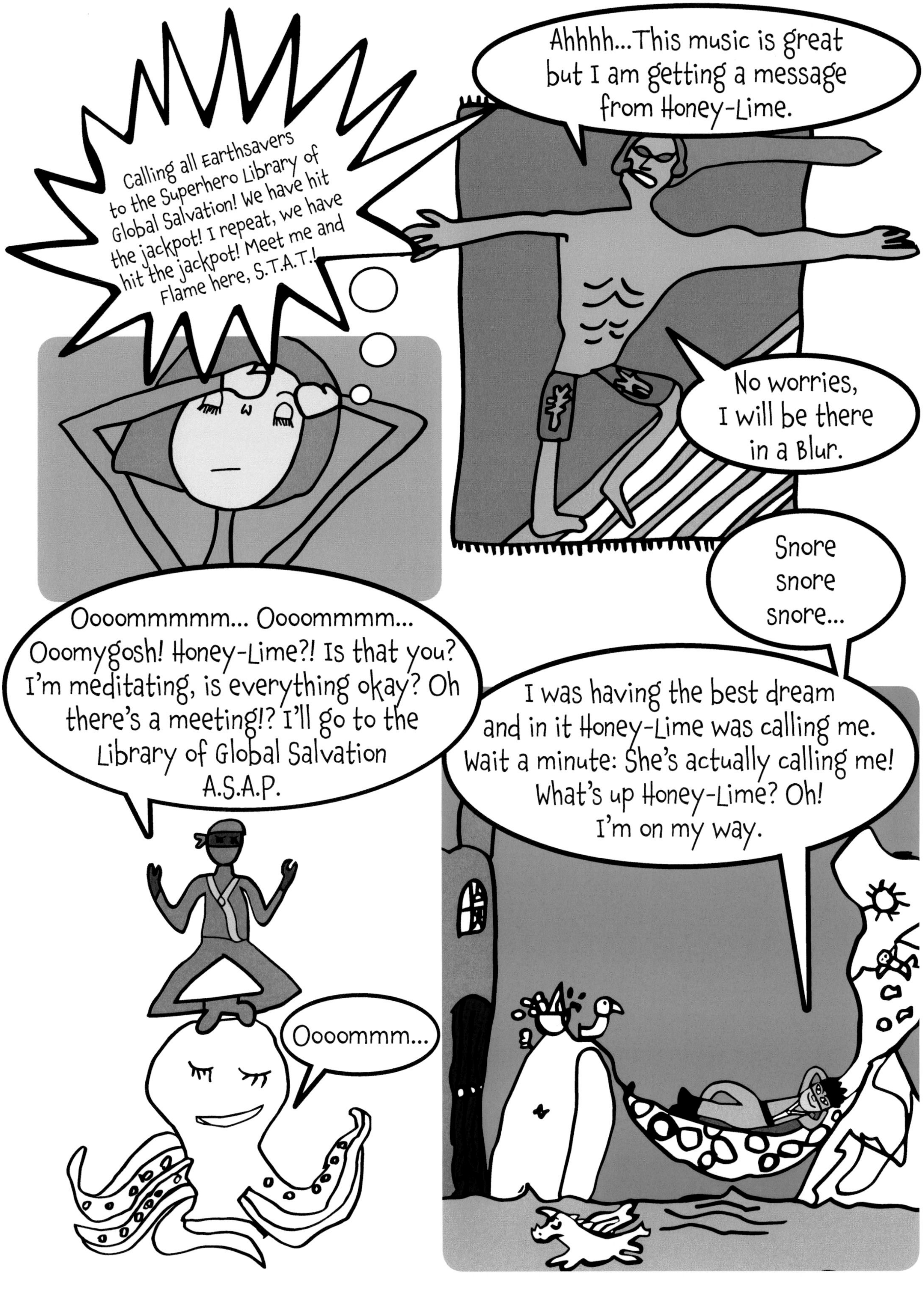

Calling all Earthsavers to the Superhero Library of Global Salvation! We have hit the jackpot! I repeat, we have hit the jackpot! Meet me and Flame here, S.T.A.T.!
Ahhhh...This music is great but I am getting a message from Honey-Lime.
No worries, I will be there in a Blur.
Oooommmmm... Oooommmm... Ooomygosh! Honey-Lime?! Is that you? I'm meditating, is everything okay? Oh there's a meeting!? I'll go to the Library of Global Salvation A.S.A.P.
Oooommm...
Snore snore snore...
I was having the best dream and in it Honey-Lime was calling me. Wait a minute: She's actually calling me! What's up Honey-Lime? Oh! I'm on my way.

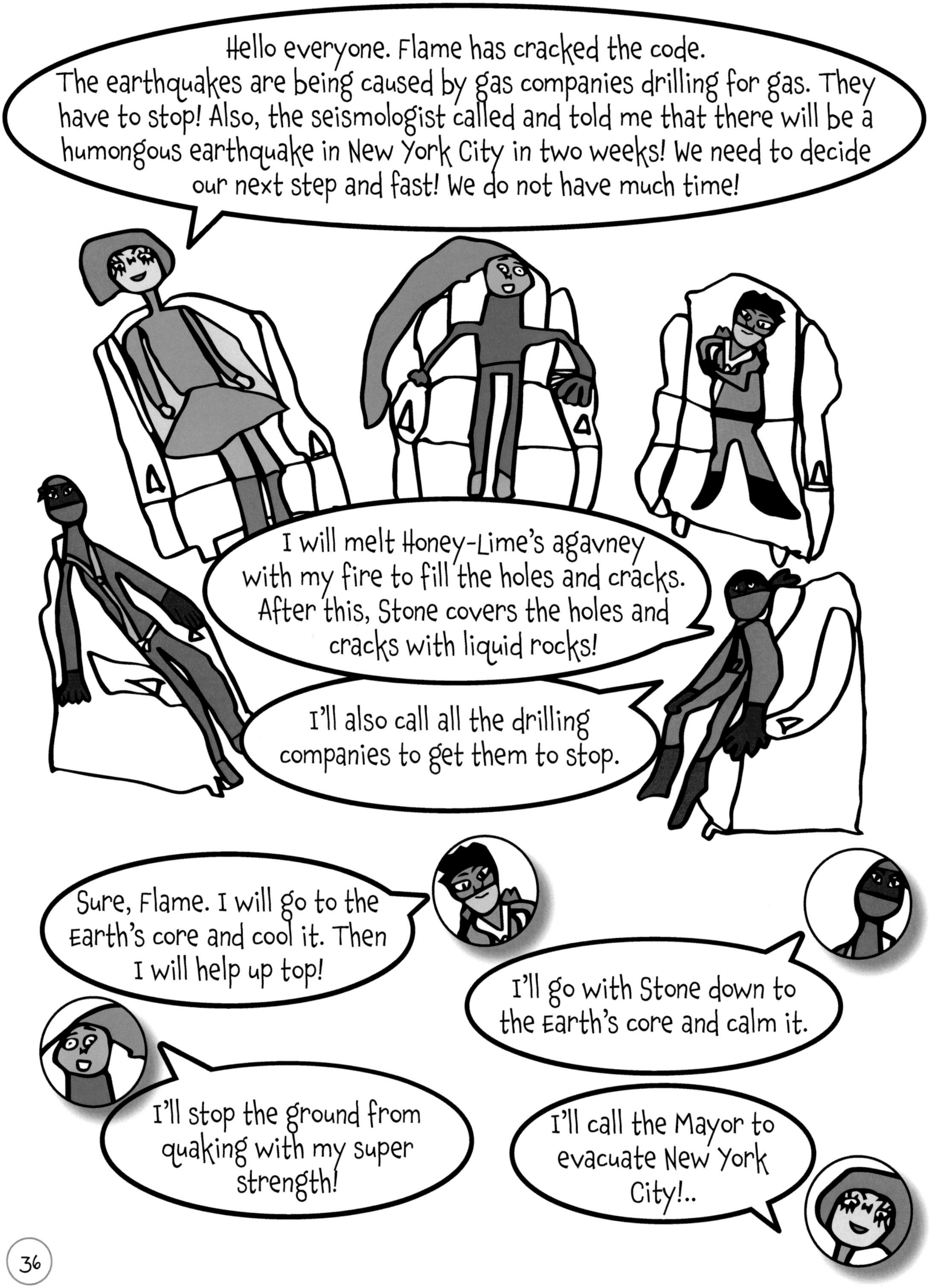
Hello everyone. Flame has cracked the code. The earthquakes are being caused by gas companies drilling for gas. They have to stop! Also, the seismologist called and told me that there will be a humongous earthquake in New York City in two weeks! We need to decide our next step and fast! We do not have much time!
I will melt Honey-Lime's agavney with my fire to fill the holes and cracks. After this, Stone covers the holes and cracks with liquid rocks!
I'll also call all the drilling companies to get them to stop.
Sure, Flame. I will go to the Earth's core and cool it. Then I will help up top!
I'll go with Stone down to the Earth's core and calm it.
I'll stop the ground from quaking with my super strength!
I'll call the Mayor to evacuate New York City!..

Chapter #7
The Big Bang!

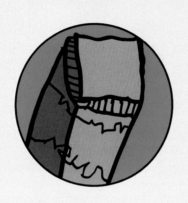

NYC is being evacuated...

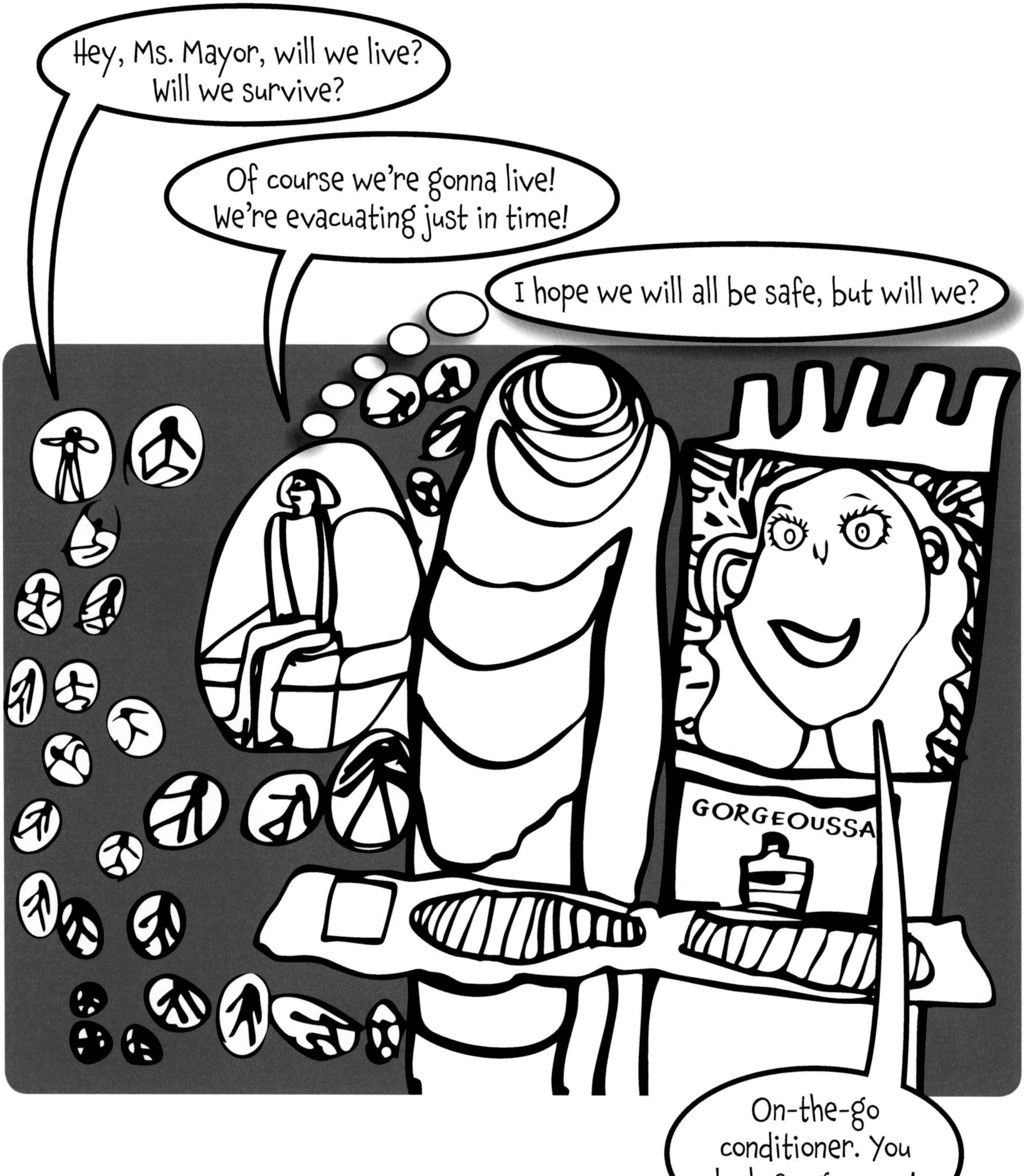
Hey, Ms. Mayor, will we live? Will we survive?
Of course we're gonna live! We're evacuating just in time!
I hope we will all be safe, but will we?
GORGEOUSSA
On-the-go conditioner. You look Gorgeoussa!

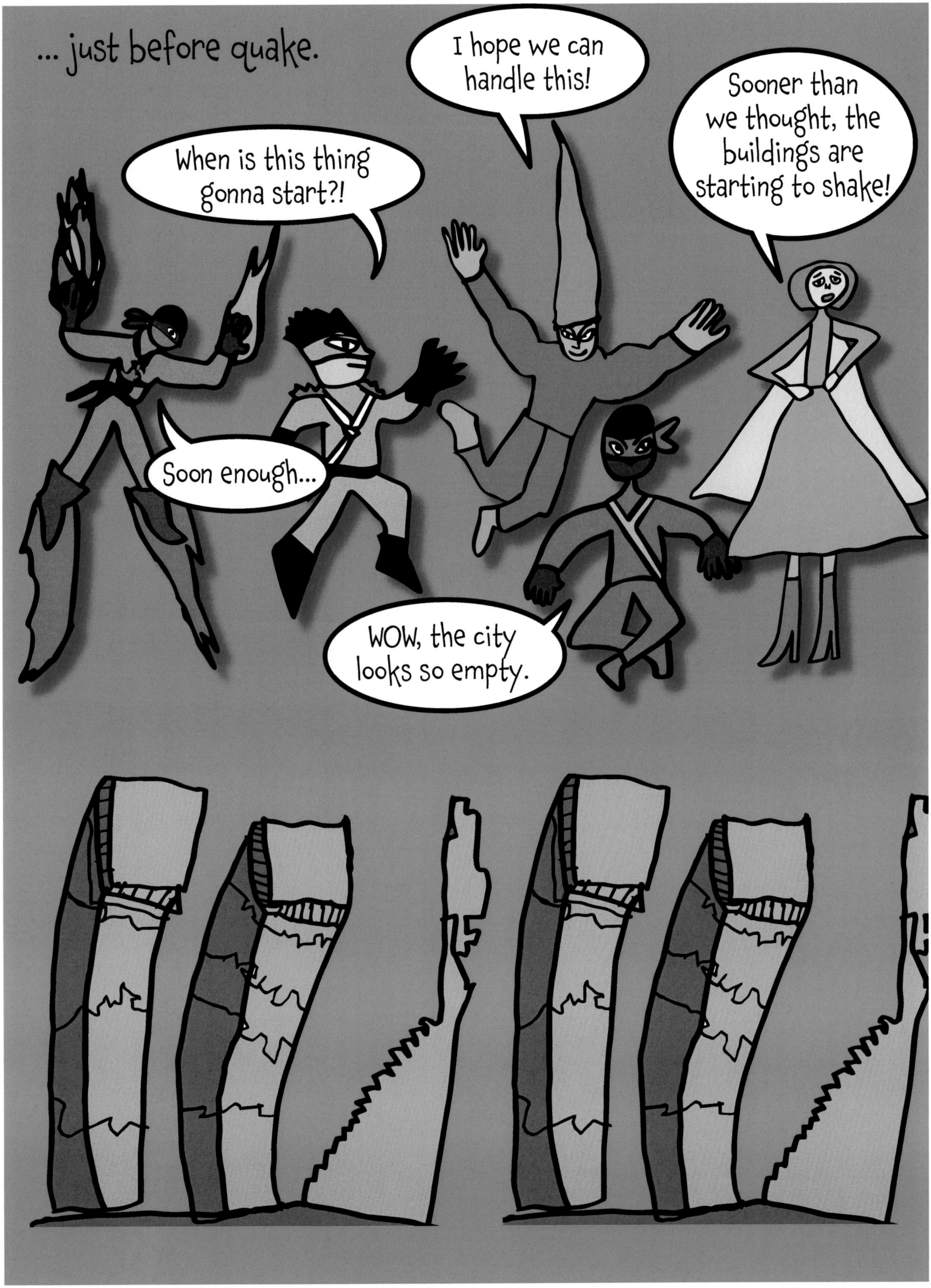

... just before quake.
When is this thing gonna start?!
Soon enough...
I hope we can handle this!
Sooner than we thought, the buildings are starting to shake!
WOW, the city looks so empty.

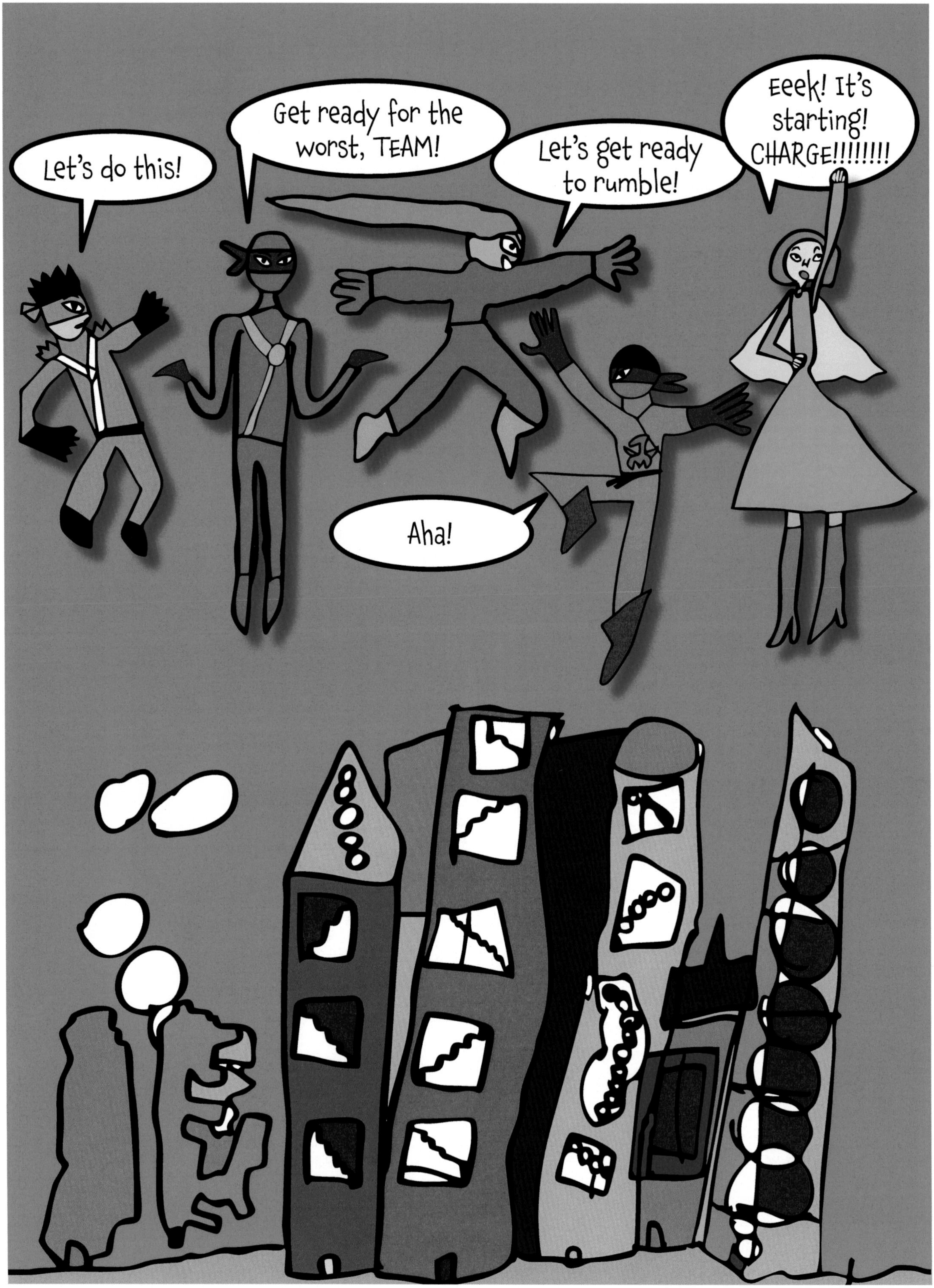
Let's do this!
Get ready for the worst, TEAM!
Let's get ready to rumble!
Eeek! It's starting! CHARGE!!!!!!!!!
Aha!

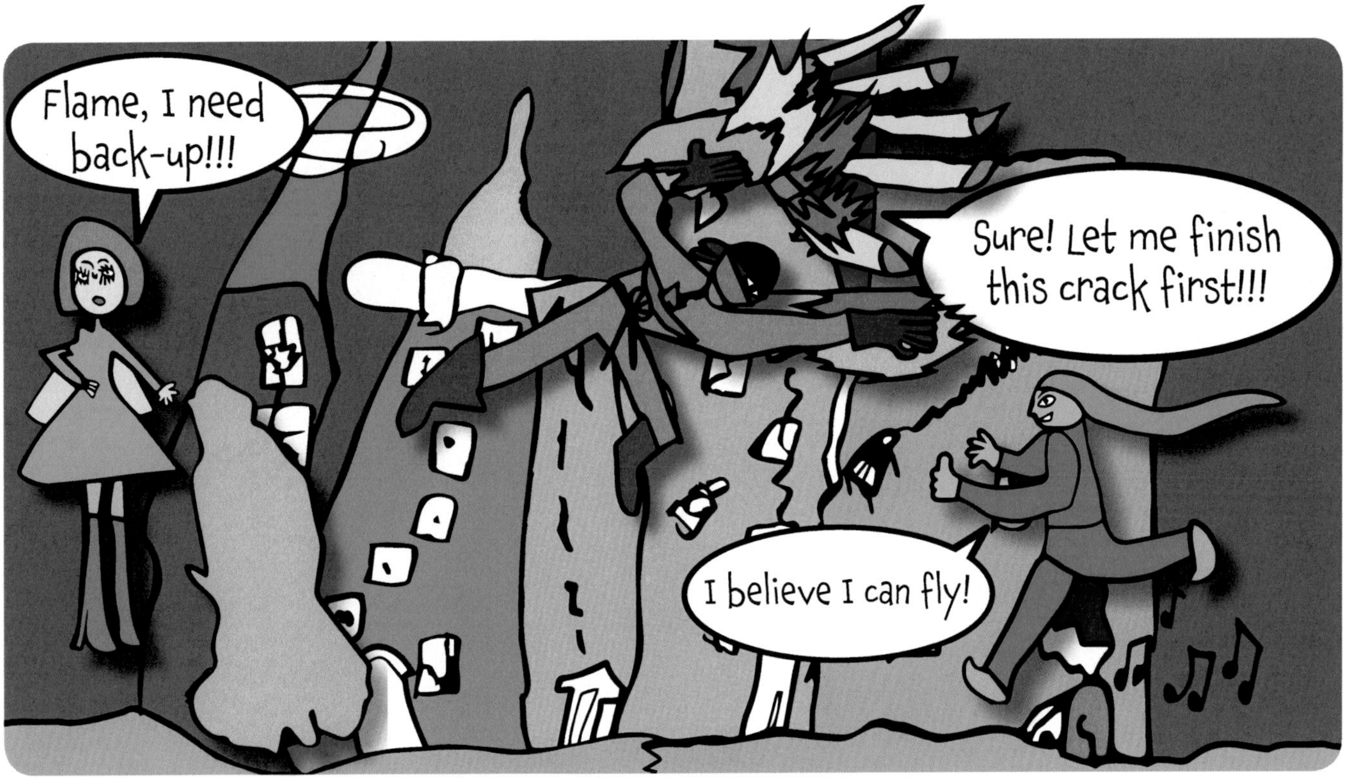
Flame, I need back-up!!!
Sure! Let me finish this crack first!!!
I believe I can fly!

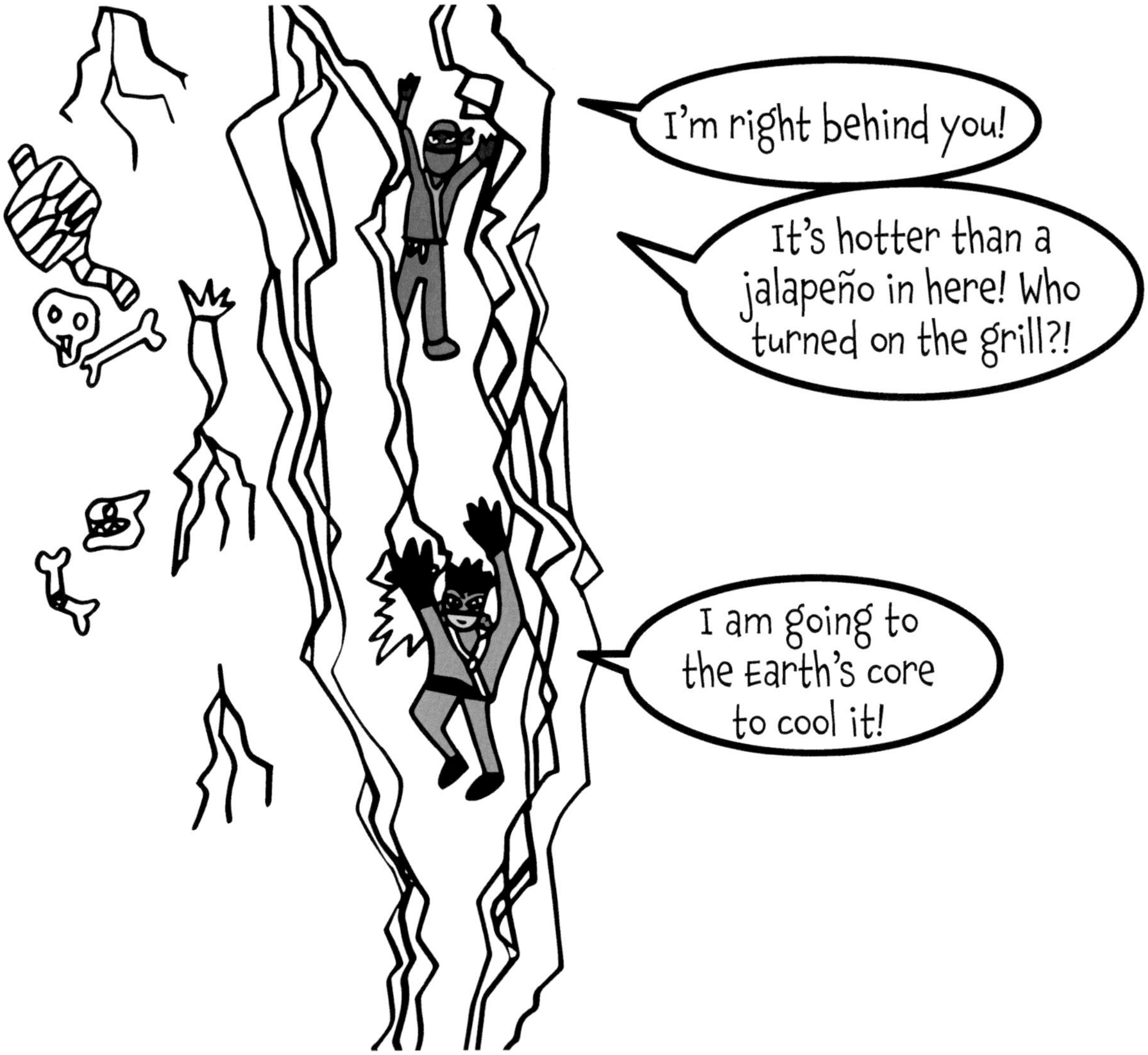
I'm right behind you!
It's hotter than a jalapeño in here! Who turned on the grill?!
I am going to the Earth's core to cool it!

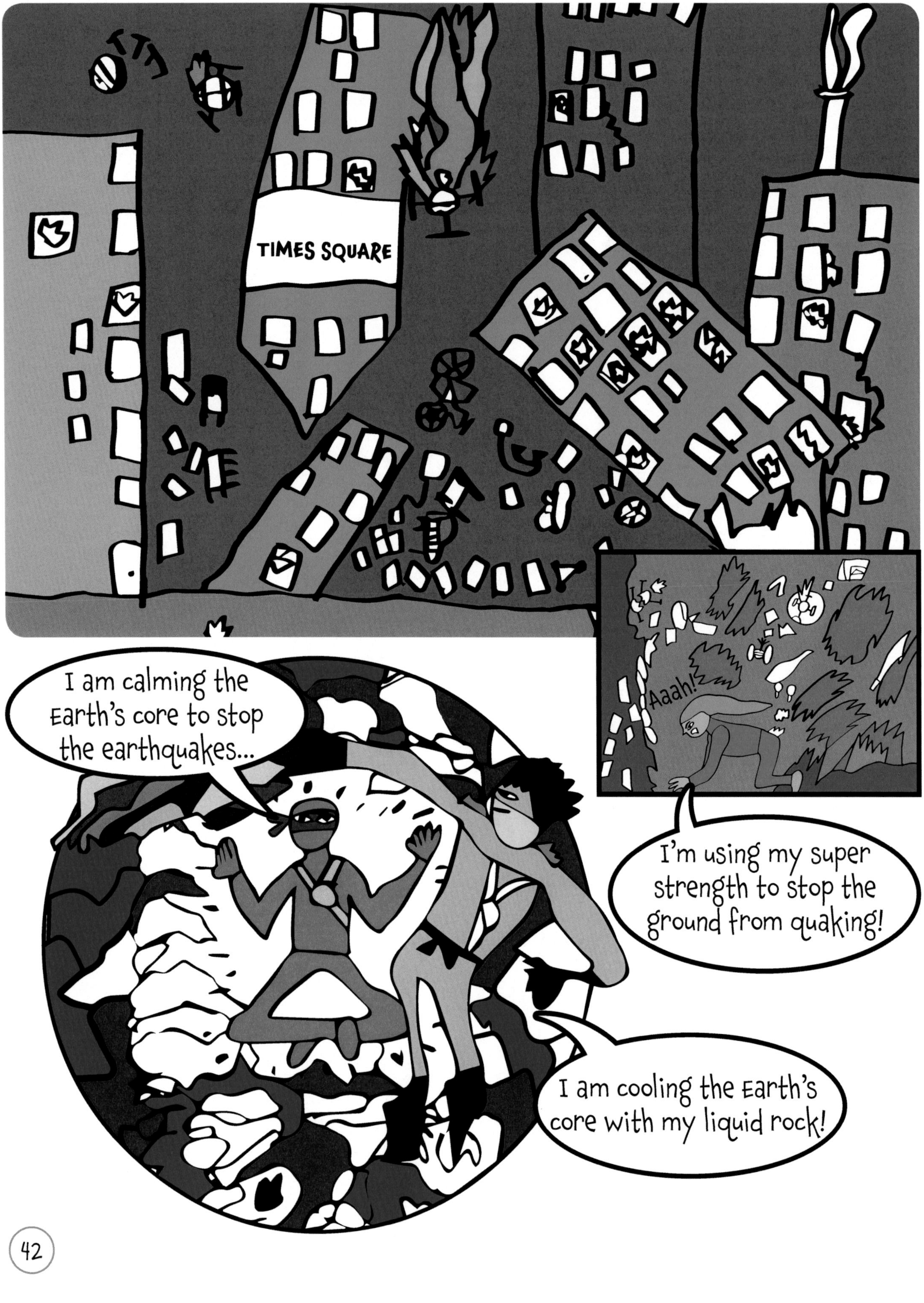

TIMES SQUARE
Aaah!
I am calming the Earth's core to stop the earthquakes...
I'm using my super strength to stop the ground from quaking!
I am cooling the Earth's core with my liquid rock!

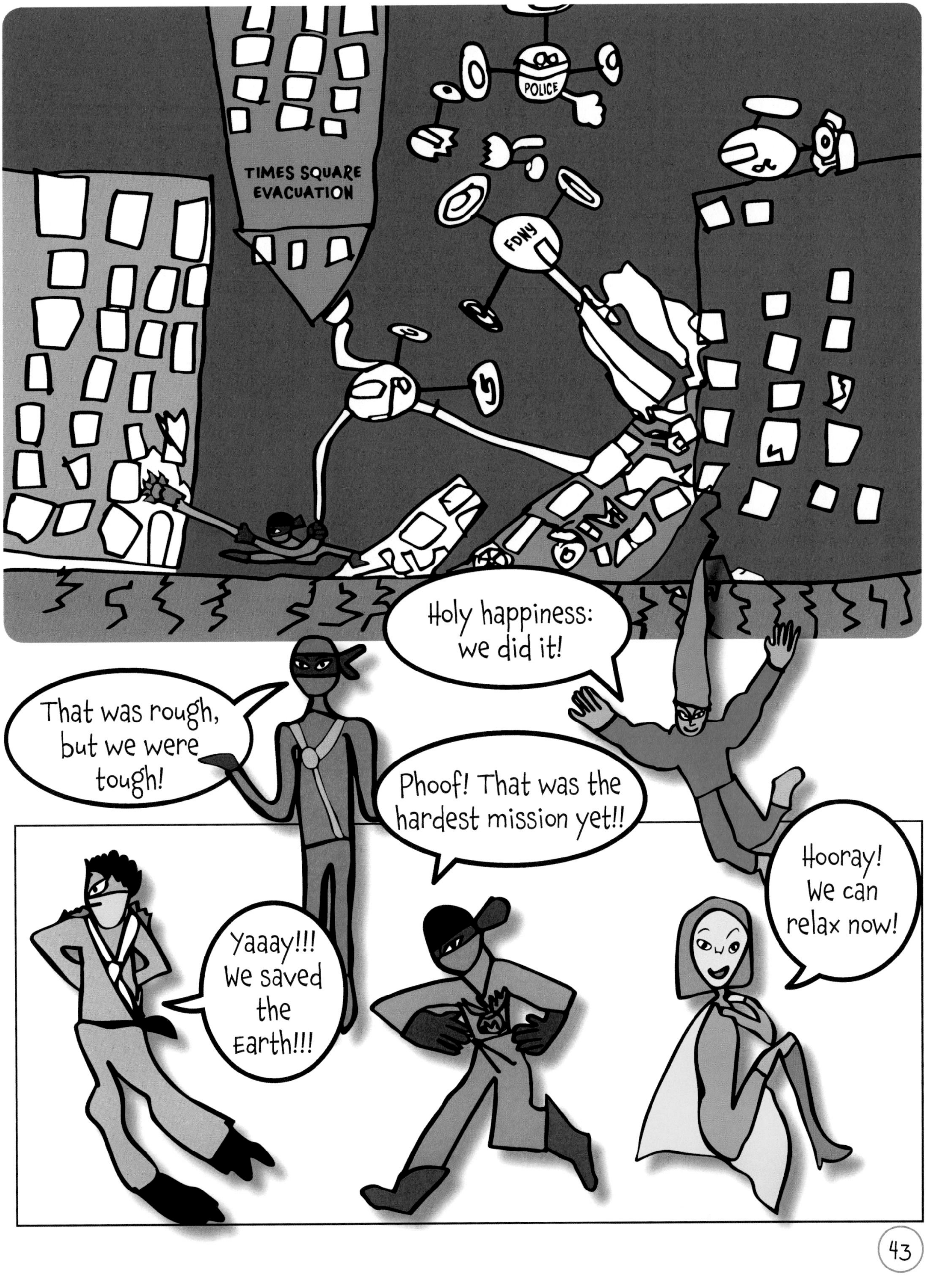
TIMES SQUARE EVACUATION
POLICE
FDNY
Holy happiness: we did it!
That was rough, but we were tough!
Phoof! That was the hardest mission yet!!
Hooray! We can relax now!
Yaaay!!! We saved the Earth!!!

Chapter #8
The New Hope!

Earthsavers,
Heroes of
The Earth

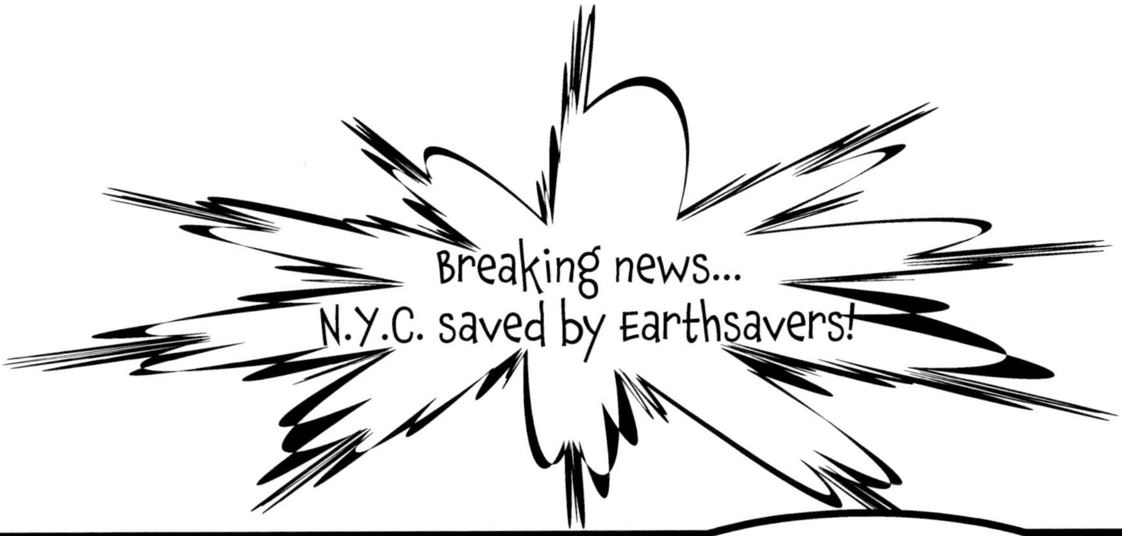
Breaking news...
N.Y.C. saved by Earthsavers!

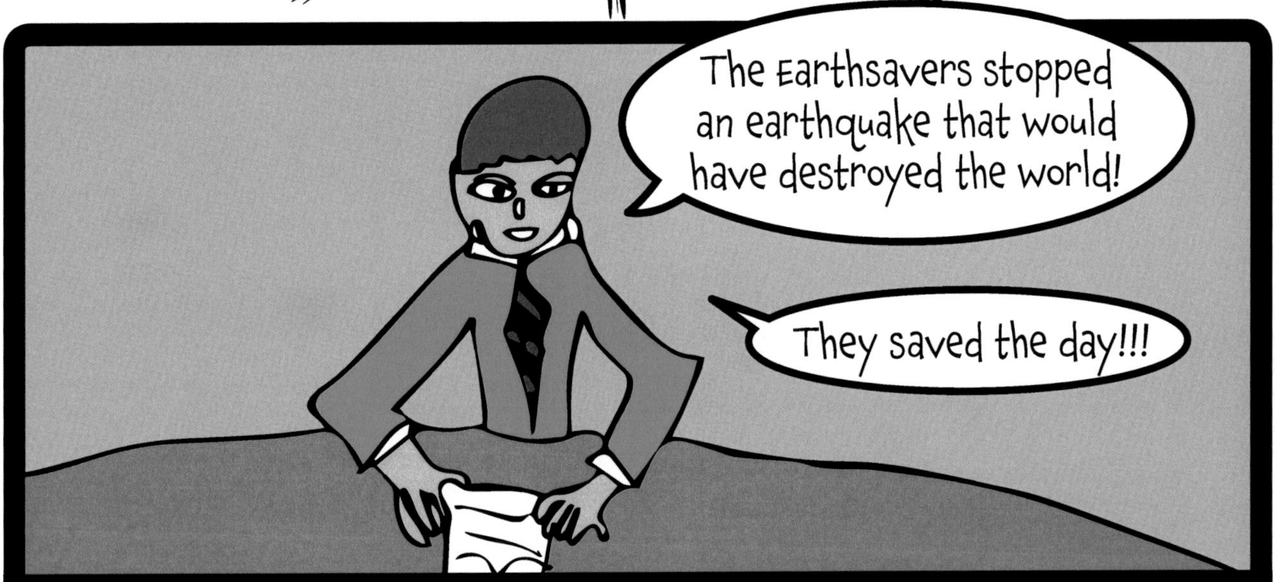
The Earthsavers stopped an earthquake that would have destroyed the world!
They saved the day!!!

The world celebrates what could be the narrowest escape in history!

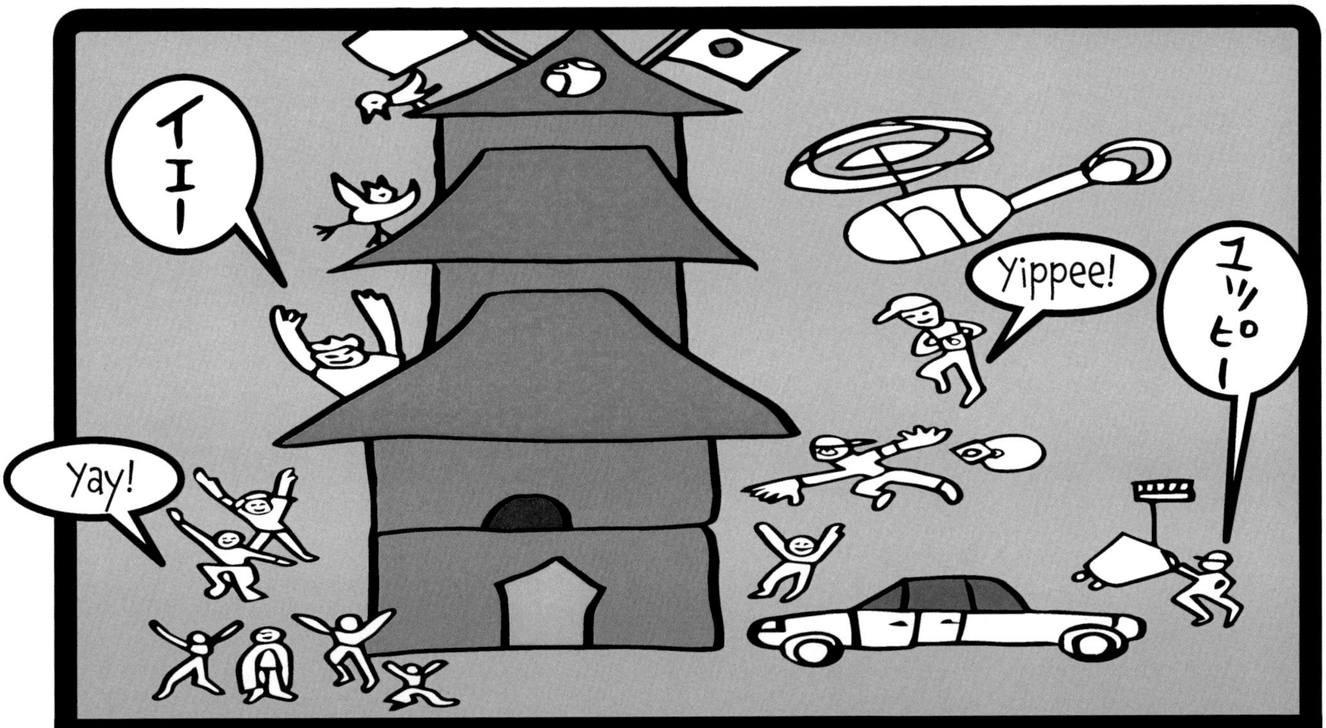
イエー
Yippee!
ユッピー
Yay!

In Tokyo, Japan people jump for joy.

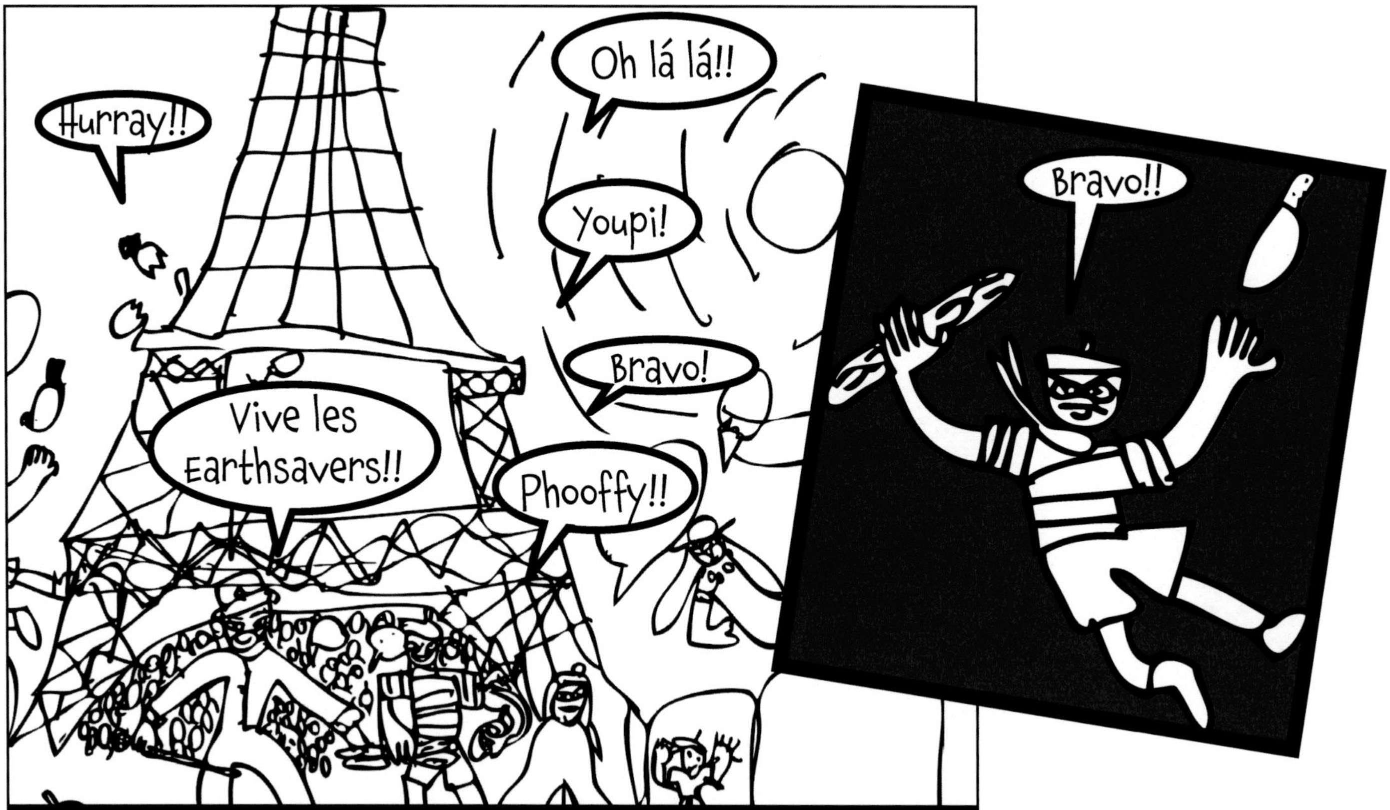
Hurray!!
Oh lá lá!!
Youpi!
Bravo!
Vive les Earthsavers!!
Phooffy!!
Bravo!!
In Paris, France people throw baguettes.

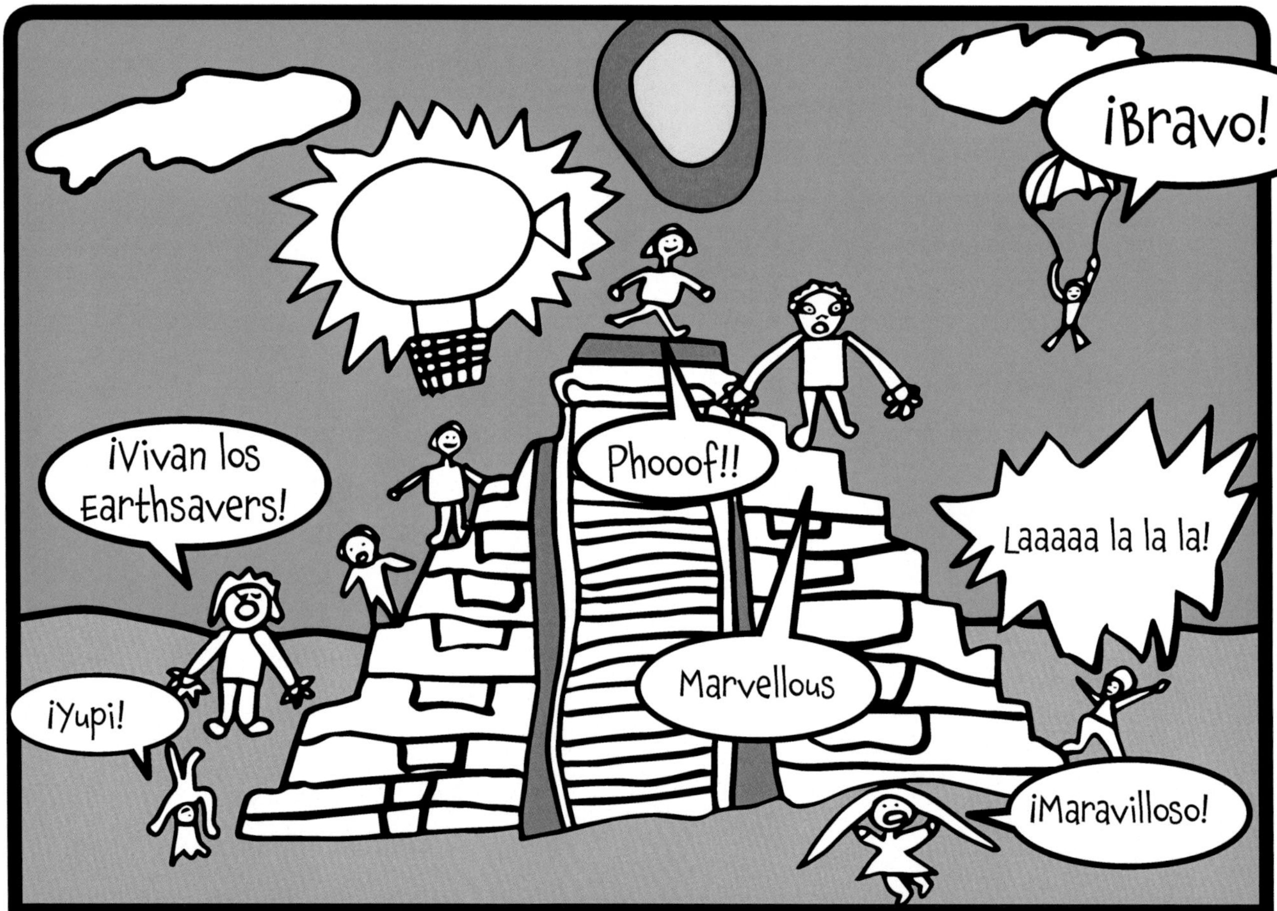
¡Bravo!
¡Vivan los Earthsavers!
Phooof!!
Laaaaa la la la!
Marvellous
¡Yupi!
¡Maravilloso!
In the Yucatan, Mexico, people cheer and sing.

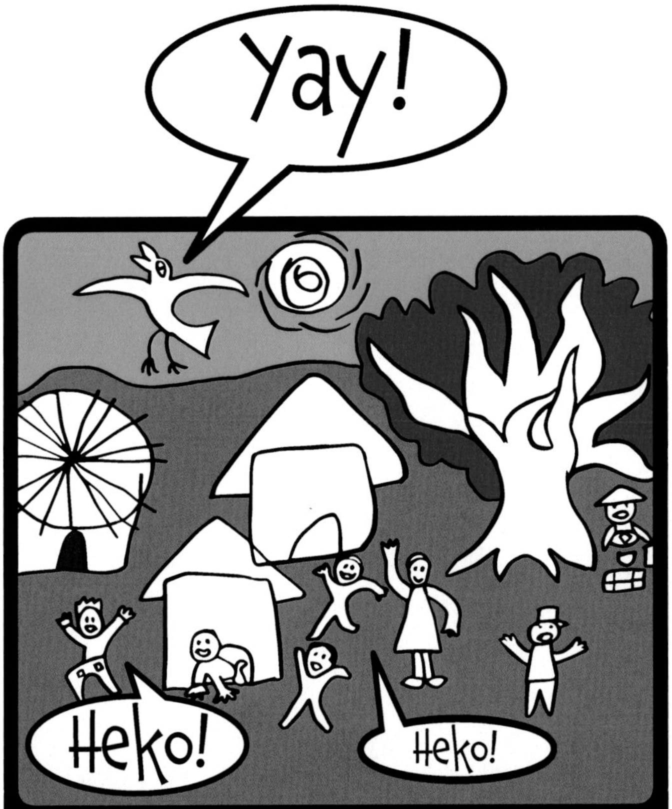
Yay!
Heko!
Heko!

In Kenya, people dance and picnic.

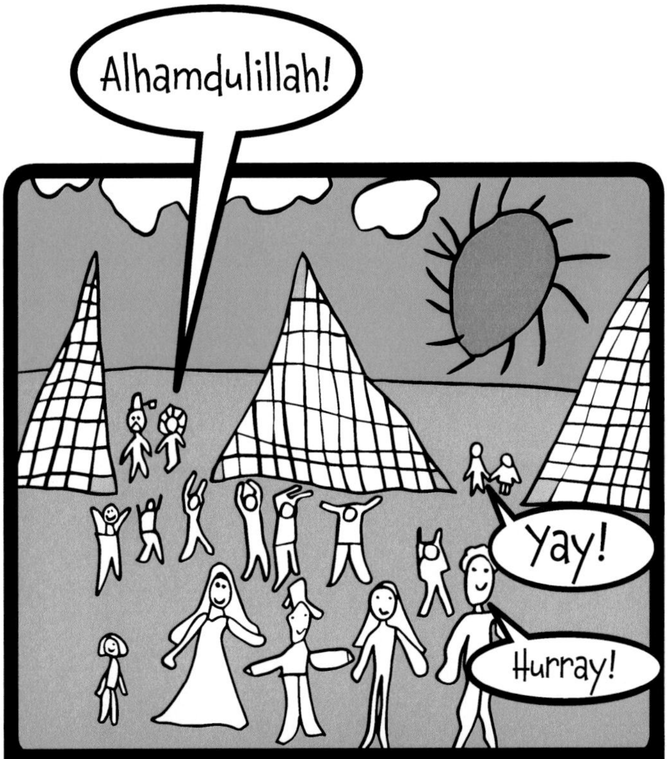
Alhamdulillah!
Yay!
Hurray!

In Giza, Egypt people chant and wave.

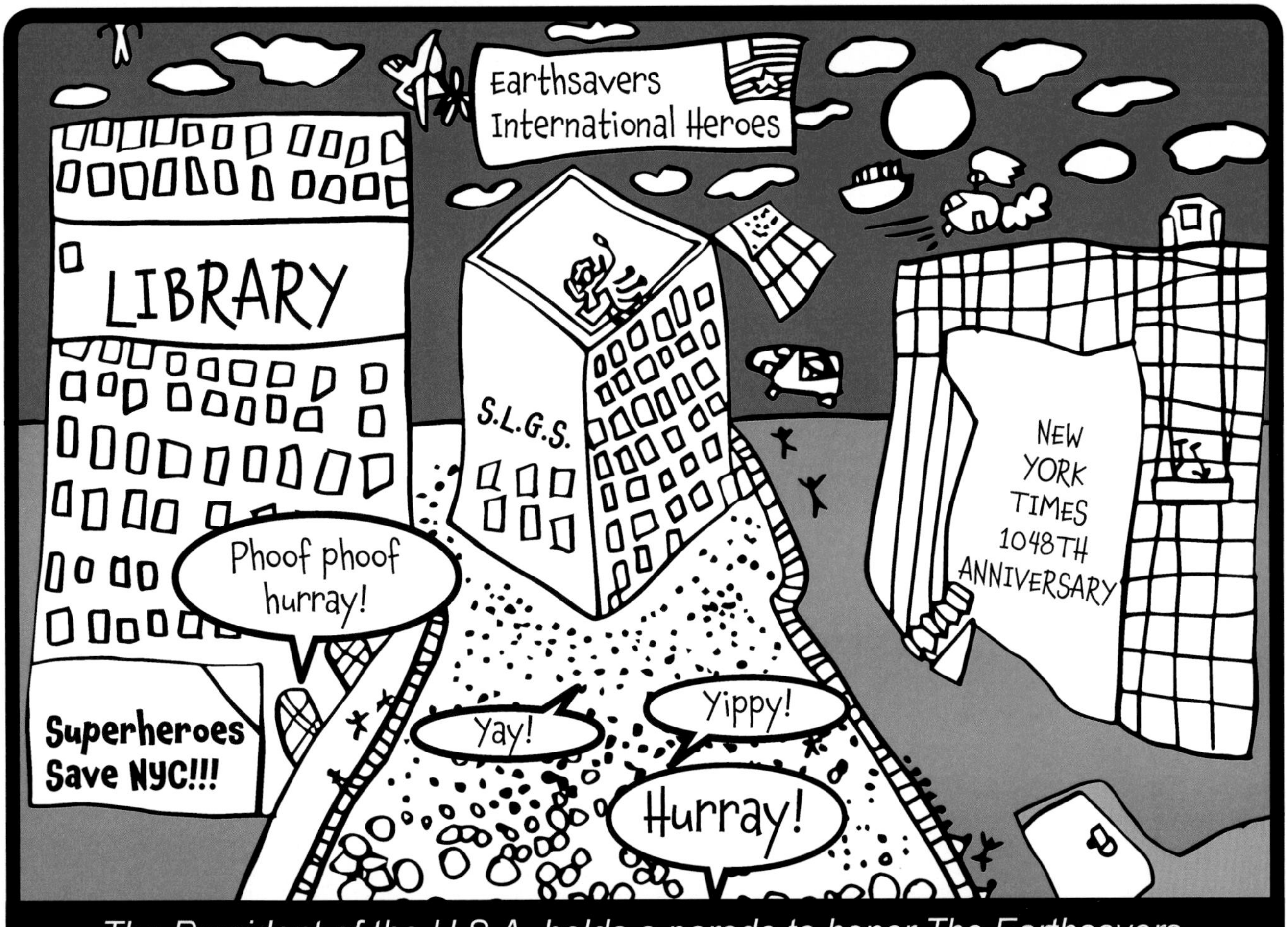
Earthsavers International Heroes
LIBRARY
S.L.G.S.
NEW YORK TIMES 1048TH ANNIVERSARY
Phoof phoof hurray!
Superheroes Save NYC!!!
Yay!
Yippy!
Hurray!

The President of the U.S.A. holds a parade to honor The Earthsavers.

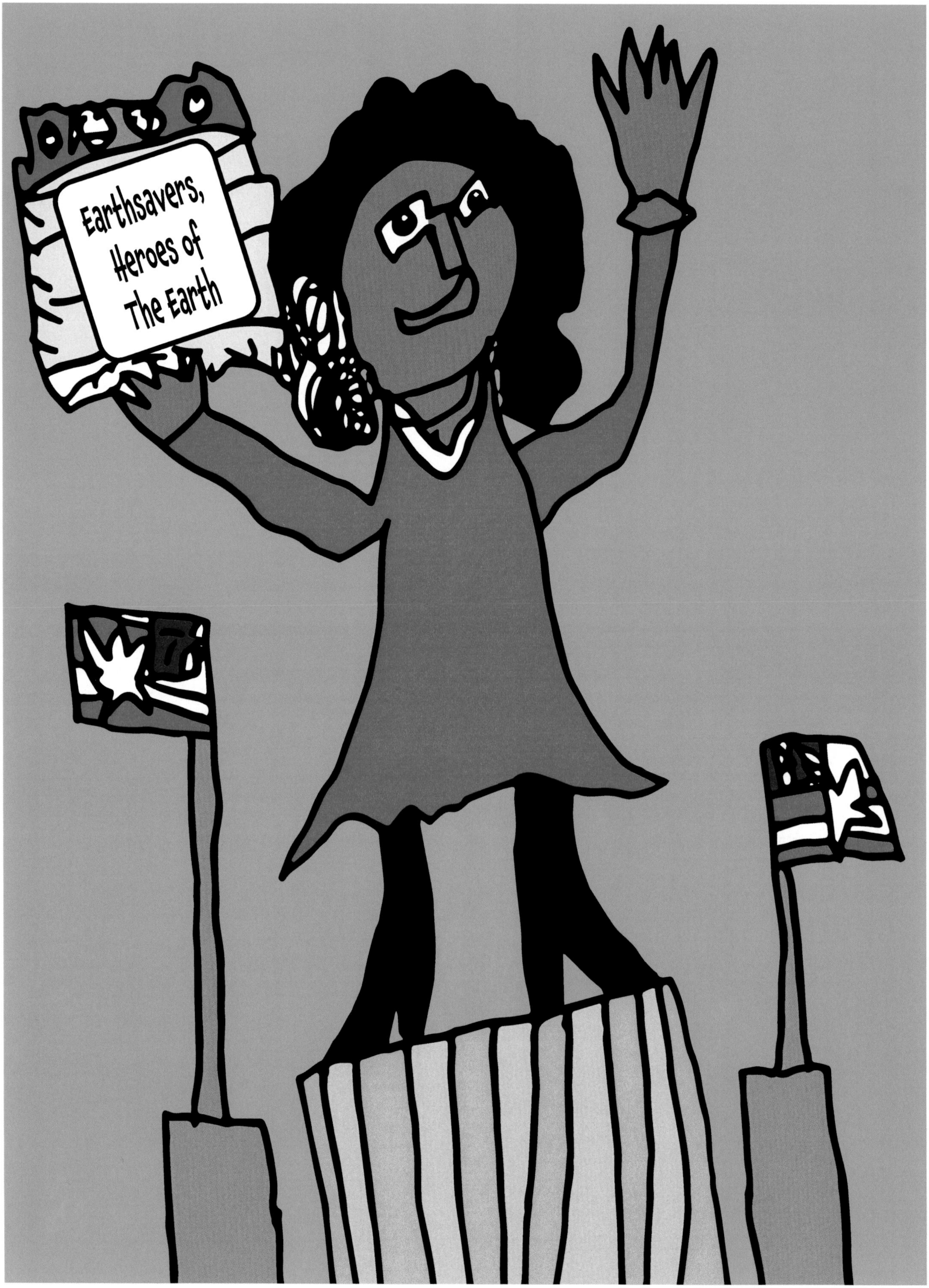
Earthsavers,
Heroes of
The Earth

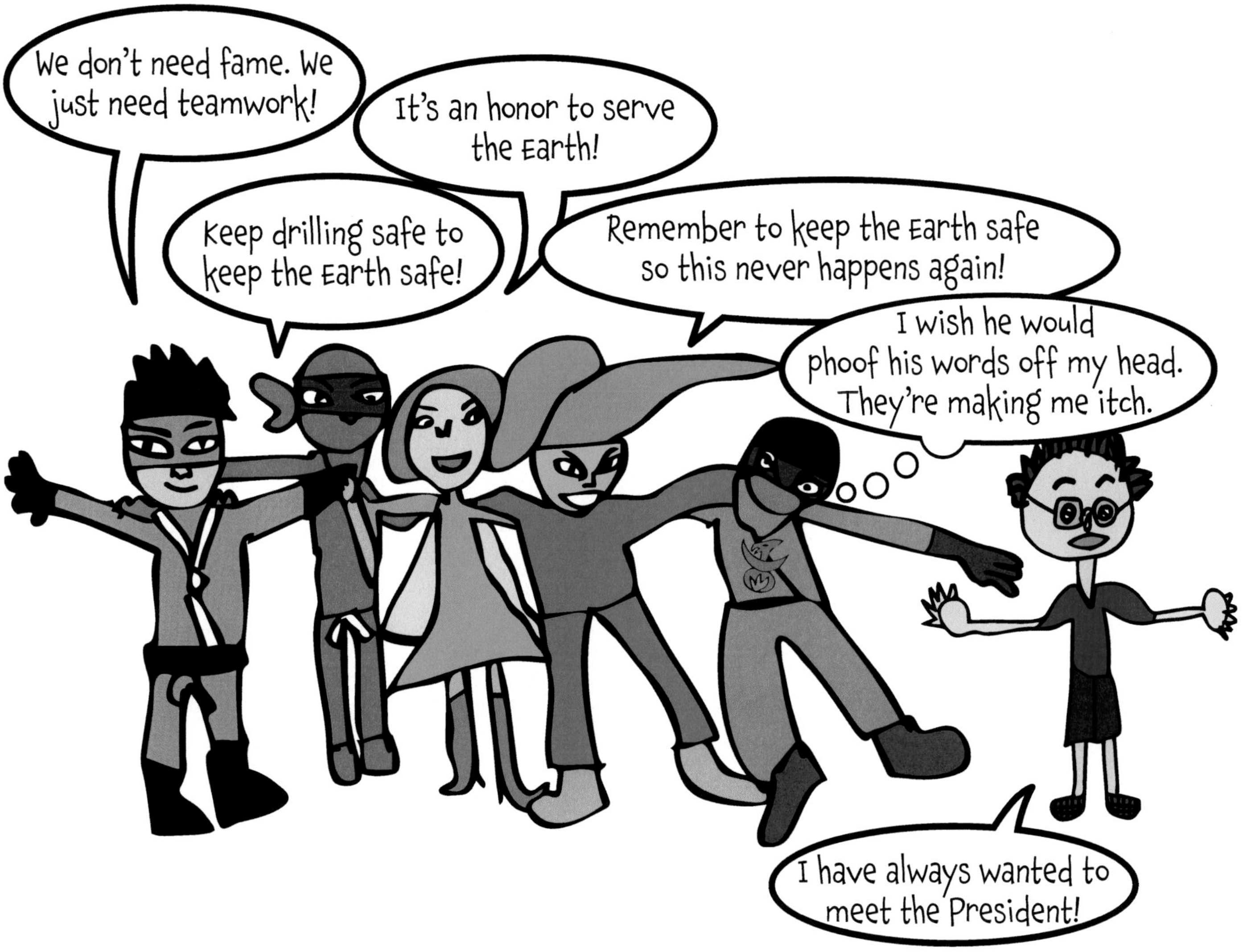
We don't need fame. We just need teamwork!
It's an honor to serve the Earth!
Keep drilling safe to keep the Earth safe!
Remember to keep the Earth safe so this never happens again!
I wish he would phoof his words off my head. They're making me itch.
I have always wanted to meet the President!

All's well that ends well was the way this story ended. The gas companies stopped drilling for gas and vowed to find other ways to create fuel and make money. All the damage the earthquake caused has been repaired like it never happened, and everyone is safe and has happily moved back into their homes. So, as you can see, this story has a happy ending or, should we say, a happy beginning?

The End

About the Authors

Sulaf Hatab

Sulaf Hatab is a nine-year-old girl who writes articles and short stories in her spare time and has been one of the principle players, thanks to her talent for dancing and singing, of every Pono production since the beginning of time. She loves cosmetics, books, arts and crafts, and her parents, who have, in her words, "always supported me throughout the difficult comic-book-making process" (she loves her parents much more than the former). In this book, she is "Honey-Lime". She thanks her teachers, Julietta, Bek, Magnolia, and Poppy, and her friends and fellow Earthsavers: "This whole thing would have been a pile of baloney without all of you; you are awesome!"

Towa Moriyama Mikami

Towa Mikami is a curious ten-year-old boy who likes reading, writing, sketching and physical activity; that is why he decided to be a part of the comic book. The comic book was later to be a musical. Self titled, "Guy-who-doesn't-like-to-talk-too-much," he is also surprisingly a good actor and poet! He created the character, "Flame" in this book. He thanks the people who helped him in the process, such as Bek Millhouse and Julietta Eisenberg.

Claudio Narciso

Claudio Narciso is an eight-year-old boy. He is half American and half Italian (right now he feels more Italian). He likes to play soccer but this summer is learning how to do a lot of cool dive moves in the swimming pool. His character is "Blur", and he is the strongest character of all (he got his idea from The Hulk).

Matteo Narciso

Matteo Narciso is a ten-year-old boy. Claudio is his younger brother. Like Claudio, he is half American and half Italian. He is very good at soccer and he plays in a travel team in New York. The character that he created for the Pono comic book is "Kai" and - fun fact - Matteo loves to read Italian comic books, all the time, everywhere!

Aure Ruiz Halpert

Aure (A.K.A. Roly) Ruiz Halpert is a creative nine-year-old boy. He loves to invent things, and he's very curious. He loves creating drawings, 3D art, gadgets, imaginary worlds, songs and dramatic characters. He created the character "Stone" in this comic book. He lives in the Bronx with his mom and dad, and loves his school.

Jasper Stoneberg

Jasper Atticus Stoneberg is a ten-year-old boy living in Inwood and Harlem, NYC. He has two cats named Nina Eldert Simone-Cherry Garcia, and Sir William Xenos. He has a phobia of water bugs. He is a New York City subway maven and a language aficionado. The "Dr. Kale" character was his brainchild.

Julietta Eisenberg

Julietta Eisenberg is a veteran teacher of language, literacy, drama, poetry, and song-writing. She is also a poet, singer/song-writer, and dancer. Sharing her love of creative expression with Pono's children by mentoring them through the process of producing this book has been a source of great joy and inspiration for her. Drawing on her super powers of creative concept envisioning and development, along with both literacy and drawing instruction, Julietta is secretly the invisible seventh Earthsaver, known to some as "Word Woman"!

Bek Millhouse

Bek Millhouse is an award-winning children's book illustrator and graphic designer. The Earthsavers is her fourth "book-baby". She manages a diverse design portfolio and happily divides her time between her book projects, commissions and her richly observed paintings. She aspires to create imagery that address social and environmental needs. Bek has inhabited the High Sierra, the Outback and now calls the metropolis of New York City home. Find her full story on Instagram @bekmillhouse.

Note: Pono would like to acknowledge the additional artistic mentorship of Magnolia Porter and Poppy Luca during the initial stages of this project.

Pono's educational program was founded in 2010
in New York City by a parent, educator, and education
researcher in response to the need for an alternative
school option that protects children's innate curiosity,
genius, wonderment, and drive to explore and grow, by
trusting them to initiate and direct their own learning.

To learn more about Pono, visit our website
(www.pono.nyc) or follow Pono's news on
Facebook (facebook.com/pononyc),
Instagram (@pono.nyc),
and Twitter (@pononyc).

pono

A journey to becoming
balanced human beings